The
Universal
Multiplication
of Intelligence

The Better Baby Press

Philadelphia, Pennsylvania

The Universal Multiplication of Intelligence

Glenn Doman
J. Michael Armentrout
and
The Staff
of
The Institutes for the Achievement
of
Human Potential

The authors wish to thank the publishers of Time for their kind permission to quote from copyright material:

Time, Vol. LXXI No. 2 (January 11, 1963), p. 48

Reprinted by permission from TIME, The Weekly Newsmagazine; Copyright Time Inc. 1963.

Library of Congress Cataloging in Publication Data

Doman, Glenn
Armentrout, J. Michael
    The universal multiplication of intelligence
        1. Intelligence—Increasing (Preschool)
    2. Child development I. Title
                    80-66236

ISBN: 0-936676-02-7

"Men fear thought," says Bertrand Russell, "as they fear nothing else on earth—more than ruin, more even than death." But in every age since the pyramid builders', there have been a few exceptional men who would willingly risk death for the enjoyment of thinking. Whether Socrates had as high an I.Q. as Shakespeare or Descartes, Schweitzer or Einstein, will never be known. What is certain is that all such men used their brains as energetically as they knew how. Today, man may have no greater brain capacity than the ancients, but he has revolutionary ideas about how to exploit it.

From all-out education, it is but a step to "complete neurological organization," in which the individual will be guided to exploit the potential of both his brain hemispheres, instead of leaving one of them largely dormant. This is the aim of neurologists, educators and other researchers, who are now organizing a group of Institutes for the Achievement of Human Potential. If they succeed, they will produce the Bacons of the 20th century—equally at home in computer theory and the kitchen garden, in the nucleus of the atom and all recorded literature.

Time, January 11, 1963

Section I
how to use this book

This book is divided into several sections in recognition of the fact that even those readers who might be vitally interested in its content may not have time to read everything we have written.

For those readers who have 60 seconds to devote to the subject of multiplying the intelligence of children, we recommend that you read "Precis", SECTION I.

For those readers who have several minutes to devote to the subject of multiplying the intelligence of children, we recommend that you read "Foreword", SECTION I.

For those readers who have half an hour to devote to the subject of multiplying the intelligence of children and wish to learn what our full plan is to accomplish this goal, we recommend that you read "Foreword", SECTION I and

"Procedure for the Individual Multiplication of Intelligence", "Procedure for *The Universal Multiplication of Intelligence*" and *"UMI* Method" in SECTION III, The Present.

Finally, for those readers who wish to have the full background of how we were led to this Plan plus the full content of the Plan itself and its postulated results, we recommend that you read the entire book and the references given in "Appendix C", SECTION VI, Table of References.

table of contents

foreword

The work of The Institutes for the Achievement of Human Potential has thus far spanned the forty year period which began in 1940.

By 1980 it had covered 135 nations and every continent except Antarctica.

It had dealt in the most intimate way with more than ten thousand families and with their children who ranged from profoundly brain-injured to average and beyond.

It had studied children in every culture from the most primitive cultures of Jungle, Desert or Arctic to the most civilized in the world.

It had devoured the lives of hundreds of Staff members, including some of the greatest people of the Twentieth Century.

It has been well worth the price of the lives it has consumed.

The work of the people of The Institutes for the Achievement of Human Potential has produced knowledge which is literally incredible and the importance of which is incalculable to the present children of the world and to the future of Mankind.

The Board of Directors and the Staff of The Institutes are determined to make this knowledge available to the parents of the world, as well as the philosophy, methods and techniques necessary for its employment.

The Vollmer Foundation has witnessed the results of the application of this knowledge and recognizes it to be both true and of incalculable value to the future of Mankind.

The Vollmer Foundation has, as a result, granted to The Institutes the funds necessary to prepare a Plan whereby this precious knowledge may be utilized by families, groups or nations. This book contains that Plan. It can be employed by a single family or by a population of eight hundred million to multiply the intellectual, physical and social abilities of the people within that group.

Precisely what is this knowledge?

The work of The Institutes has made it crystal clear that it is not only possible to *multiply* the intellectual, physical, artistic, creative and social abilities of children between birth and six years of age but that doing so is more joyous and satisfying for both mother and child than are the present practices of child rearing.

How important is this knowledge?

Is there *any* more important topic to which man can turn his attention than to the subject of his own potential? Perhaps man's most ancient dream is the heady idea that he might not only change the world around him, which he has done at an almost unbelievable rate, but indeed change himself in significant ways and markedly for the better.

The fact is that we need no longer wait upon a thousand genetic accidents occurring in the majestic millions of years by which geological time is measured, but instead now have the knowledge of how to take the first steps along a purposeful, rather than accidental, road to Man's improvement of his own human condition.

What will be the result of raising all of our children to be intellectually, physically and socially superior to the present condition of our children?

It is difficult at the very best, or more likely impossible, to state what the results of this Plan will be, not because it is difficult to predict what will result but rather because the results will be overwhelmingly good. The problem therefore is one of stating the precise truth, as we presently see the truth, and being disbelieved since the enormousness of the truth is literally incredible. Should we on the other hand diminish the truth and therefore distort it in order to be believable? Is a distortion of the truth in order to make it acceptable by its diminution, more truthful than the unvarnished statement of a clear but as yet unaccomplished achievement of an inherent potential?

Herbert Spencer once stated a thought which at once was both overwhelming and devastating. He said, "The profoundest of all infidelities is the fear that the truth will be bad."

We conclude that we must state the result as we see the result, whether it is wise to do so or whether it is not. Perhaps it is even wise to do so since by doing so it is likely that we will automatically eliminate all those readers who would prefer to cling to a present reality, which is acceptable only because it is familiar, without regard to its catastrophic result in human, economic and social terms rather than to embrace a provable but as yet unfamiliar alternative which is demonstrably superior as well as more economical in human, financial and social terms.

It would be foolish indeed to prepare a Plan in such a way as to make it more acceptable to those among us who in any event would not support it or might even oppose it.

"Men fear thought as they fear nothing else on earth —more than ruin, more even than death."
Russell

This Plan is therefore written for that relative minority of people who are not frightened by the prospect of an immensely better future and who welcome the possibility that we can improve ourselves immensely at a fraction of the present cost.

> *"But in every age since the pyramid builders there have*
> *been a few exceptional men who would willingly risk*
> *death for the enjoyment of thinking."*
>
> Time, January 11, 1963

It is to these few men and women that this Plan is addressed.

Finally, before the actual listing of the results themselves, we should like to remind these few men and women to whom this Plan is addressed that there is no question whatsoever as to what the results will be in the individual children with whom it will deal. Those results will be both superb and clear since we have already produced them thousands of times in individuals and several times in groups.

> *"If they . . . (The Institutes) . . . succeed they will*
> *produce the Bacons of the 20th century——equally at*
> *home in computer theory and the kitchen garden, in the*
> *nucleus of the atom and all recorded literature."*
>
> Time, January 11, 1963

We *have* succeeded.

The children of The Evan Thomas Institute and The International School are the living proof of that prophecy made by the Medical

Editor of *Time* magazine almost two decades ago.

The Universal Multiplication of Intelligence **Plan** will literally raise markedly the quality of life on earth. It will reverse the almost insane plunge of the world's school system, the results of which are plummeting in almost inverse proportion to the skyrocketing cost of maintaining them.

It will reverse the deterioration of the family group and make that group stronger than ever in the past.

It will save millions of dollars almost immediately and create billions of dollars in the long pull.

It will in addition, by raising the intelligence of a given population, produce new ideas, goods, services and money presently beyond knowing.

The most important result of all will be a new generation of people, more capable, more energetic, more ingenious, more courageous and more determined to create a more successful and more humane world than ever before.

The only questions which remain are, which group of people will first have the intelligence, the concern, the imagination, the love for its children and the courage to put this Plan into effect and to reap the rich rewards it will offer for such a small and certain investment. The only other question is how quickly will other governing bodies be wise enough to observe the result and astute enough to adopt the Plan for their own children until the multiplication of intelligence is universal.

precis

PLAN:	*The Universal Multiplication of Intelligence*
FAMILIAR NAME:	*UMI*
OBJECTIVE:	To multiply the intelligence of the world's population by increasing the intelligence of every newborn baby during the first three years of life while simultaneously strengthening family ties.
METHOD:	To teach every mother of a newborn child in a given population how to teach her baby to read, do mathematics, acquire vast amounts of encyclopedic knowledge on a host of subjects including art, biology, anatomy, history,

music, foreign languages, science, geography, zoology, botany and numerous other subjects. She will also learn how to make her baby physically and socially superior. This combination of visual, auditory and tactile stimulation, which is sensory in nature, combined with the motor functions of mobility, manual and language competence actually results in physical growth of the tiny child's brain. Simultaneously the acquisition of vast amounts of *related* sets of information permits the child to combine and permutate such bits of intelligence into knowledge which is literally beyond counting. This in turn results in the ability to determine laws by the organization of related facts. This results in a huge increase in intelligence.

BACKGROUND: The Staff of The Institutes for the Achievement of

Human Potential have spent more than forty years in studying the brain growth and development of children from conception onward. This study has included tens of thousands of children in more than 135 countries ranging from the most primitive cultures of Jungle and Desert, through the Arctic and to the most civilized cultures of both ancient and modern times.

They have worked on the most intimate basis with more than ten thousand families from more than thirty-five nations to actually significantly raise the abilities of their children in intellectual, physical and social terms.

RESULT: This Plan will result not only in the raising of intelligence by an average of fifty points but will also result in the elimination of reading problems and of learning problems. Such results would warrant the tripling of educational costs. They will instead sharply *reduce* educational costs.

COST: The costs of carrying out this Plan will range from a total cost of $300 per child in a population of 500 newborns to a cost of $180 per child in a population of ten million newborns (1979).

Section II

The Past

the major objectives

The Objectives already accomplished
by The Institutes from 1939 to the
present which led to the Plan for
The Universal Multiplication of Intelligence

THE FORTIES

OBJECTIVE ONE
(1939 to 1947)

To find a very small number of specialists highly skilled in various branches of knowledge including brain function, child development, anthropology, education, medicine, psychology, nursing, and others.

Result

This was accomplished during the years 1939 to 1947.

OBJECTIVE TWO
(1947 to 1950)

The formation of the group of specialists into a research team to explore child development and brain function.

Result

This was accomplished during the years 1947 to 1950.

THE FIFTIES

OBJECTIVE THREE
(1950 to 1955)

To study normal child development as the basis
for a statement of objectives for profoundly
brain-injured children.

Result
*This was accomplished during the years 1950 to
1955.*

OBJECTIVE FOUR
(1950 to 1955)

The establishment of a non-profit federally tax-exempt institution chartered in Pennsylvania with the stated purpose of "conducting research, training and treatment, the objective of which is to raise the abilities of all brain-injured human beings". This institution to be known as "The Rehabilitation Center at Philadelphia".

Result

This was accomplished in May of 1955 with the chartering of "The Rehabilitation Center at Philadelphia" as a non-profit institution in the Commonwealth of Pennsylvania. The name would be changed to "The Institutes for the Achievement of Human Potential" in 1962 and the objective modified to embrace the improvement of well children to higher levels of intellectual, physical, and social accomplishment.

OBJECTIVE FIVE
(1955 to 1962)

To discover the means of increasing the brain-growth and function of brain-injured children in order to make them able to function normally in intellectual, physical, and social terms.

Result
This was accomplished during the years 1955 to 1962.

THE SIXTIES

OBJECTIVE SIX
(1962)

To change the name of the organization to "The Institutes for the Achievement of Human Potential" and to change the objective to that of "conducting research, teaching, and training as to how to raise the ability of *all* human beings to perform in the intellectual, physical, and social realms."

Result

In 1962 the name of the organization was officially changed to "The Institutes for the Achievement of Human Potential" and the objective changed to embrace "the significant improvement of the abilities of all *children in the intellectual, physical, and social realms." Both State and Federal approval were granted.*

OBJECTIVE SEVEN
(1962 to the present time)

To study brain growth and development in normal children from conception through the prenatal, natal, and postnatal periods until the brain growth is essentially complete at six years of age. To study this process in more than 135 nations and on every continent. This study to include the most primitive cultures from the Xinguanos in Brazil, the Bushmen in the Kalahari Desert, the Papuans in New Guinea to the Masai, the Eskimos, the Polynesians, the Micronesians, the Melanesians, the Africans, the Australians and others as well as children in the world's most advanced cultures. These studies to include visits to, and extensive conversations with, authorities on Man himself including Raymond Dart, Konrad Lorenz, Louis Leakey, Robert Ardrey, Linus Pauling, Boris Klosovskii, David Krech and a host of others.

Result

Beginning in the year 1962 and continuing through the present day, The Institutes have conducted innumerable expeditions, study and working visits to cultures in more than 135 nations to study children on every continent. The studies include conceptual, prena-

tal, natal, postnatal, and child rearing practices. These studies are conducted through The Institute of Man which is one of The Institutes for the Achievement of Human Potential and is headed by Professor Raymond A. Dart who occupies The United Steelworkers of America—Chair of Anthropology.

OBJECTIVE EIGHT
(1963)

To study how it had been possible to bring children with millions or even billions of dead brain cells and who had been paralysed and considered to be hopelessly mentally retarded, to levels of performance which equalled or even exceeded the capabilities of average children, including many who could read at two years of age, while fully one third of the children who were considered normal were unable to read at six or older.

Result
This was accomplished during the year 1963.

OBJECTIVE NINE
(1964)

To write a book to teach mothers how to teach their babies to read with total understanding and to achieve great joy and increased intelligence in the process.

Result

In May of 1964 How To Teach Your Baby To Read *was published by Random House and to the present date (1979) has sold more than one million copies in hardback and has been published in fourteen foreign editions including Afrikaans, Greek, Hebrew and Japanese.*

This has resulted in letters from thousands of mothers the world over, telling of their triumphs in teaching their babies to read, the joy that both mother and tiny child experienced in the process and the intellectual, visual, language and social progress their babies had experienced in learning to read.

These letters and the records of The Institutes constitute the greatest body of evidence in existence in the world today which proves conclusively that tiny children are falling far short of their inherent potential.

OBJECTIVE TEN
(1964 to the present time)

To add the knowledge of how the brain grows in average children which the team had gained to the knowledge of how to actually stimulate brain growth in laboratory animals which the world's neurophysiologists had gained. Classic examples of the work of neurophysiologists can be found in the studies of Boris Klosovskii and David Krech. Their research involving sensory deprivation and sensory enrichment conclusively proved that the brains of laboratory animals literally grow by sensory stimulation. The product of the combined knowledge would be the ability to actually grow children's brains in a physical and intellectual sense.

Result

This specific knowledge has been acquired from the year 1964 to the present time.

The result is the knowledge that:
The world has looked at brain growth and human development as if these were a predestined and unalterable fact. The truth is that brain growth and human development are a dynamic and ever changing process. This is a process which can be stopped, this is a process

which can be slowed, but most significantly this is a process which can be speeded.

All that needs to be done to speed the process of brain growth and human development is to give the tiny child visual, auditory, and tactile stimulation with increased frequency, intensity and duration, in recognition of the orderly way in which the brain grows.

By the year 1965 our knowledge of human brain growth and superiority had advanced to the point where we could enunciate the following philosophy:

THE INSTITUTES' PHILOSOPHY

PROLOGUE

The conceptual and philosophical statement set forth below is the culmination of more than 20 years experience. It is intended as a simple and straightforward declaration of what the authors believe.

During the decade of the 1930's, Temple Fay, an extraordinary neurosurgeon and scientist, developed certain basic insights concerning malfunction of the human central nervous system and concerning pragmatic treatment techniques. In 1941, Dr. Fay became the mentor of Glenn Doman, and in the years immediately following Warld War II other staff members came under his influence.

In the period of the late 1940's little had been done to fill in between Fay's notable insights and the techniques he had developed. Since 1946, the staff have worked to expand Fay's early insights into well founded concepts and the early techniques into successful treatment methods.

Works such as those of the late David Krech of the University of California, Joseph Altman of the Massachusetts Institute of Technology, and the late B. N. Klosovskii in Russia, as well as those of cyberneticist Norbert Wiener, recently of the Massachusetts Institute of Technology and of engineer James Reswick of The Case Institute of Technology, Cleveland, have provided increasing confirmation of the research findings, and they have led to a greater understanding of why the techniques, methods, principles and concepts fit together to form what can now be considered a general philosophy based on principles of neurological organization.

STATEMENT

While the process of education begins at six or seven years in most civilized nations, the process of learning begins in utero.

The learning process of an individual begins in utero. It begins long before the moment of birth and possibly at the instant of conception. The learning process is clearly evident with the birth cry as the baby begins to breathe air for the first time, in the new environment, outside his mother's body.

From the instant of birth onward the learning process takes place at what can be described only as a breathtaking pace.

It is possible that the child learns more, fact for fact, before he enters school than he will learn thereafter in the rest of his life.

By six, he has learned about himself, his relationship with his family, his family's relationship with its community, and his community's relationship to the larger world.

He has learned about individual ownership, family ownership, community ownership, and national ownership.

He has learned about words, phrases, sentences, and he has learned the better part of an entire language.

He has learned about how to move his bodily parts, and he has learned about how to crawl, creep, walk, and run.

He thinks abstractly and is sophisticated about a world which deals in terms of nuclear energy and space travel.

This very small listing of accomplishments does not begin to touch the scope of the child's learning achievements. It is after all of this, that we normally say he is ready for the process of formal education.

The process of formal education is, in the end, nothing more than the transmission of existing information from the teacher to the pupil, coupled with presentation of a degree of love for the subject —— that is, assuming that the teacher has proved worthy of identification as a teacher.

When, in the presentation of this philosophy, we use the term learning, we mean it in the broadest sense, encompassing the entire process. By learning how to hear while in utero, how to distinguish light from dark at two days of age, how it feels to use arms and legs in crawling at one week of age, how to understand spoken sentences at eighteen months of age, how to read and deal with abstractions and thus eventually, how to achieve the highest level of human learning and thereby performance as a consequence.

DEVELOPMENT

Learning is a function of the central nervous system. A review of the literature on learning evokes this pronouncement as the only generalized truth about learning on which there is universal agreement. There is also broad agreement on the idea that the more complex the nervous system the greater the ability of the organism to learn more completely and more abstractly.

PHYLOGENETIC DEVELOPMENT

The relationship of complexity of function is demonstrated in those creatures of the earth that have developed more complex nervous systems as they developed more complex functions. "You may be sure that first there was a need and then there was a facility. Nature is an opportunist" (Fay).

Man represents the present peak of phylogenetic rise in the size, complexity and organization of the central nervous system, a process which has spanned millions of years. He also represents the present peak among all living creatures in his ability to learn.

As one descends in the animal kingdom through less complex central nervous systems, the successively lower creatures may be said to have successively lower learning abilities as compared with higher forms of life.

The ability to learn correlates directly with development of the nervous system. This relationship results in a high learning ability in well-developed nervous systems and a low learning ability in undeveloped or underdeveloped nervous systems. This is also true *within* a species and nowhere is the difference between individuals as evident as it is in man himself.

A primary function of the brain is to relate the organism to its environment. It is axiomatic that the central nervous system of an organism develops through use. Although the neurophysiological evidence to support this view is manifold, few examples are clearer than that of Klosovskii's newborn kittens and puppies. After 10 to 19 days of rotation in a horizontal plane, the experimental animals showed 22.8 to 35 percent increase in the size of the vestibular areas of the brain as compared with the control animals.

ONTOGENETIC DEVELOPMENT

Development of the brain is a result of interaction of the organism with its environment.

Increased interaction produces increased development and decreased interaction results in decreased development. This interaction, which is prerequisite to development, is also prerequisite to learning.

Assuming physical integrity of the brain, we have seen that the brain interacts with its environment through a cybernetic loop which begins in the environment, follows afferent or sensory pathways to the brain and then efferent or motor pathways from the brain back to the environment. Thus, information about the environment, as it reaches the brain through sensory pathways, is the primary prerequisite for development of the central nervous system, and, as a result, for learning.

HUMAN SENSORY GROWTH

Variations of environmental opportunity result in variations of the informational nourishment upon which sensory pathways of the brain grow, are elaborated and are organized. Such variations range from severe sensory deprivation to enormous sensory enrichment. These variations in quantity and quality of the environmental input account for growth of the sensory pathways.

Building and elaboration of sensory engrams takes place as a result of correlation of the myriad stimuli received by the brain as well as a result of the intensity, frequency, and duration with which the stimuli are applied.

Therefore growth, elaboration, and organization of the sensory pathways may be limited by a lack of stimulation and they are increased in direct relation to the frequency, intensity, and duration of sensory input.

Learning is limited to the amount of information which the brain has received and stored and the ability to learn more is limited to the amount of information the sensory pathways can process.

Since it is input that elaborates the sensory pathways and, since the amount of input which can be handled is dependent upon growth of the sensory pathways, it is obvious that the more input (and therefore learning) which takes place, the more input (and therefore learning) is possible. It is thus evident that the sensory pathways, which are the result of input, constitute the ability to learn and pure learning is the amount of information a brain has acquired.

While this kind of learning process has been long understood in a motor context, it has not been understood in a sensory context. Function determines structure in both sensory and motor terms. Biceps function, for example, creates a stronger, larger and more effective biceps. More importantly, this stronger, larger and more effective biceps is now capable of greater feats of strength, variety and effectiveness than a less functioning biceps, which in turn enables it to become still stronger, larger and more effective. In the same way, sensory input elaborates sensory pathways and such input contributes not only to the sum total of learning, which is stored but, more importantly, it makes the sensory pathways capable of even greater learning feats. A child who knows more than another child can be taught more than the other child but, more importantly, such a child is neurologically more capable than the other child.

If input is non-existent, limited or confused, the sensory pathways (and therefore learning) will similarly be undeveloped, underdeveloped or incorrectly developed. As a result, there will be no sensory function, underdeveloped sensory function or incorrect sensory function.

Conversely, if input is multiplied, varied, and clearly programmed, the sensory pathways (and therefore learning) will similarly be developed, enriched, and organized. As a result, there will be greater sensory function, enriched sensory function and organized sensory function.

Learning is a sensory process.

HUMAN MOTOR GROWTH

Information or learning which does not result in performance is obviously useless.

While learning is dependent upon the sensory pathways, performance is dependent upon the motor pathways.

It is well understood that motor pathways are developed and elaborated through use.

What has not been understood is that the building and elaboration of motor pathways is entirely dependent on the previous creation of sensory pathways. If sensory pathways are undeveloped, underdeveloped, or incorrectly developed, the motor pathways will similarly be undeveloped, underdeveloped, or incorrectly developed. As a result, there will be no motor function, underdeveloped motor function or incorrect motor function.

The influence of motor function on learning is to reinforce learning. As a consequence, if motor pathways and thus motor function are undeveloped, underdeveloped, or incorrectly developed, learning will not exist, will be incomplete, or will be incorrect to the same degree.

Development of motor pathways of the brain, and thus reinforcement of learning, takes place as the organism reacts expressively or efferently to stimuli coming from the environment through afferent pathways.

The sensory pathways and the motor pathways taken with their interconnections make up the organ known as the brain.

Learning is a function of the brain.

THE DYNAMICS OF ENVIRONMENT

The process of learning is dependent on the complexity of development and on organization of the brain. Development of the brain, in turn, depends upon opportunities of this organ to take in and react to stimuli offered by its environment. Variations in environmental stimulation result in variations in the ability to learn.

Sensory deprivation, and thus lack of expressive opportunity for reinforcement, can be the result of environmental variations. Therefore, an extremely limited environment creates a virtually zero state or idiot brain.

While a limited environment creates brains limited in both development and function, on the other hand, a highly enriched, a highly varied, a highly organized, and a highly dynamic environment results in a highly developed, versatile and highly organized brain. Environment therefore is a factor strongly at play in the development of inferior or a superior brain.

CYBERNETIC FUNCTIONS

The effect of environment (or input) upon performance (or output) can be seen clearly when one considers the almost exact functional analogy between the human brain and the computer.

Norbert Wiener developed the entirely new field of cybernetics when he saw this analogy following creation of the first electronic computer.

Henshaw has referred to the human brain as a wet system and the computer as a dry system.

INTENSITY OF INPUT

If the dry system computer is supplied with no input for storage it will give no answer. Such a computer is said to be in an unprogrammed or zero state. We have learned that the wet system or human brain when supplied with no input for storage will also give no answer and can be said to be in an unprogrammed or idiot state.

Henshaw states that if a dry system computer is given only limited input it will give back limited or unsophisticated information. Such a computer is said to be in a partially programmed state. We have learned that the wet system or human brain when supplied with limited input for storage will produce a child with limited or unsophisticated information. Such a child can be said to be in an unsophisticated or immature state.

An ordinary dry system computer given ordinary input will give back limited heuristic information —— that is, information obtained by search and discovery. Such a computer may be said to be in a limited heuristic state. We have learned that the wet system, or human brain, when supplied with average information for storage will produce a child who has average and limited heuristic information. Such a child can be said to be an average one or one with limited heuristic capability.

In order for a dry system computer to give back truly heuristic information a superior computer had to be developed. Such a computer is called an heuristic computer. We have found that a high degree of input into the wet system, which is the child's brain, does in fact create a superior system which will give back heuristic information. Such a child is regarded as a genius. Therefore, in either humans or computers which have physical integrity, the environment or input is an important determinant of performance or output.

However, a limited environment is not the only factor which can interfere with brain development. Lack of physical integrity of the brain is also a factor which can limit brain development. Such lack of physical integrity can result from trauma to the brain prenatally, natally or postnatally. This will also result in lack of performance.

INTEGRITY OF SYSTEMS

What has just been said of injured wet systems can also be said of a computer which has damage. A computer with extensive damage will give back no information. Such a computer may be said to be in a non-functioning state. A child with an extremely damaged brain will give back no information. Such a child may be said to be in a non-functioning or vegetable state.

In a high percentage of cases we can correct damaged computers by making internal repairs or readjustments. When this is done, the computer is made to function. Such a computer is said to be repaired. We have discovered that, in a high percentage of severely brain-injured children, we can correct damage by certain surgical procedures or by neurological reorganization of the child. When this is done, the child is made to function. Such a child is therefore said to be rehabilitated.

A computer which has less extensive damage will take in less information or will take in the information in a garbled way. It will therefore, give back limited information or garbled information. Such a computer may be said to have a learning problem. We have found that a child with less extensive brain damage will also take in limited information or take in information in a garbled way. Such children give back limited performance or garbled performance. Such children are also said to have learning problems.

We can correct such a computer through reorganizing it. When this is done the computer is made to function. Such a computer may be said to be organized. We have discovered that with children who have less extensive damage we often correct the problem through use of certain organizational procedures. When this is done, the child is made able to function at his appropriate level. Such a child we say is organized.

In summary, the following statements can be made about wet and dry computers.

1. When supplied with no sensory input, they will remain in an idiot state until information is supplied. Supplying information with increased frequency, intensity and duration will often correct the problem.

2. When they are able to receive no information due to extensive damage or dysorganization, they will be in a nonfunctional state until extensive reorganization is carried out by supply of information with increased frequency, intensity, and duration.

3. When supplied with limited sensory input, they will remain unsophisticated or immature until appropriate information is supplied. Supply of information with increased frequency, intensity, and duration will correct this problem also.

4. When they are able to receive only limited information, or information received in a garbled way due to less extensive damage or dysorganization, they will have learning problems until reorganization is carried out and until they are then supplied with the necessary information increased in frequency, intensity, and duration.

5. When they have ordinary physical integrity and are supplied with ordinary amounts of informational input, they respond with ordinarily expected performance.

IMPLICATIONS

When a superior computer is created based on the presently existing computer, or a superior brain is created based on enriching the input to the present brain, the result will be a highly heuristic dry system and a genius wet system.

The knowledge now exists to make dry systems highly heuristic.

Where do we stand on making the wet system genius?

After many years of failure it has been learned that the normal level of environmental stimulation is not sufficient to overcome the neurological deficit caused by environmental deprivation or by trauma to the central nervous system. It was therefore our original postulation that it might be possible to modify and heighten development of the underdeveloped or traumatized brain. This obviously could be done surgically where necessary by removal of obstacles to neurological development and organization. It obviously might be accomplished non-surgically also by enhancing the environment through a myriad of correlated stimuli greatly increased in frequency, intensity, and duration.

While knowledge that the environment plays a role in brain growth is not new, the directness of that role and the degree of its importance have been greatly underestimated. The work of David Krech with sensory enriched and sensory deprived rats makes this very clear.

Indeed in the ancient debate between the geneticists and the environmentalists as to which of these factors has the greater bearing on ultimate development of men or of man, it would now appear to the authors that man is falling so far below his environmental ceiling that genetic factors have comparatively little influence. It is our present position that not until man is reaching his environmental ceiling will the genetic differences in man be measurable as a practical matter.

PRESENT LEVEL OF KNOWLEDGE

This statement reports our present level of knowledge, based upon two decades of clinical research with several thousand "mentally retarded" or frankly brain-injured children.

The unique body of knowledge accumulated has led us to our present position.

The Institutes for the Achievement of Human Potential are now committed to a significant increase in the ability of *all* children to achieve physical, intellectual, and social excellence.

These objectives are to be obtained in all children throughout the spectrum of human accomplishment.

The Institutes have devoted much time to researching the problems of childhood behavioral development. Our methodology for this research has included both pathological and clinical deviations from expected norms of development.

Studying children who are lacking developmentally has led to the conclusion that most of the developmental lags are directly correlated with similar lags in development of nervous system. Because children who exhibit such lags progress at a slower rate than do normal children, or indeed not at all, we have been able to ascertain validly the significant developmental sequence without interference from the vagaries of the chronology of development. To this we have added the physiological correlates.

In well human beings the process of brain maturation, which begins at conception and which is clearly evident at birth, is virtually complete by six years of age.

The speed at which this process takes place varies widely from human being to human being.

By measuring children against the several functional scales which comprise *The Institutes' Developmental Profile* (the criteria by which it is possible to measure the child's level of progression in this process of brain maturation), we can determine the child's neurological age.

It can easily be established that the process of neurological maturation can be *slowed slightly* by certain cultural factors which prevent good brain organization, that this process can be slowed *considerably* by certain environmental deprivations which create neurological dysorganization, and that this process can be *completely halted* by brain injury.

The *delaying* of neurological maturation is evidenced by the *immature child* or the slow learner.

The *dysorganization* of neurological growth is evidenced in the *reading problem* or the *retarded child*.

The *total halting* of neurological growth is seen in the *severely brain-injured child*.

In a neurological sense all children can be embraced in a continuum which ranges from the severely brain-injured child without neurological organization at one end of the spectrum to the superior child with extremely good neurological organization at the other end of the spectrum.

The work of the individual institutes has established clearly, and contrary to popular belief, that children who are far below average in this continuum can be raised to average levels. Indeed, the work has proved that even severely brain-injured children may be raised to average levels by the employment of surgical or nonsurgical approaches.

When significant numbers of brain-injured children had been raised to average and, occasionally, far above average brain levels, it became apparent that *the process of neurological maturation can be speeded as well as delayed and that this speeding can be accomplished by certain simple non-surgical procedures.*

The use of these procedures on normal children has enabled us to significantly enhance developmental progress in infancy and childhood.

As a result, we can change human potential which was formerly considered a static and irrevocable fact to a dynamic and ever-changing process. In short, we may be able in the near future to improve universally the very nature of Man.

SIGNIFICANCE

Such a global concept, together with these simple procedures that are applicable on a universal scale, could be of such significant importance that their continued reassessment and indeed their dissemination to the people, need very careful and judicious scientific and lay direction.

To show the magnitude and the urgency of attention to work in this field, certain comments by Oliver J. Caldwell of the U.S. Office of Education are cited. Following a visit to Moscow in 1963 for interchange of Soviet and American ideas concerning education, programmed learning and the human mind, Dr. Caldwell wrote as follows:

> *Since my visit to Moscow, I have discussed with a number of American scholars and scientists the work being done in the United States, in the U.S.S.R., and elsewhere designed to expand the capacity of the human brain and thus to create a "superior man." It is clear that considerable re-*

search is being done in this area. However, as a nonprofessional observer, I have the impression that research in the U.S.S.R. may be more advanced than similar research in the non-Communist world. If this is true, and if the Soviet scientists achieve even a small portion of their stated goals during the next generation, the results could bring about a serious effect on the balance of power.

We were impressed by the Soviet scientists we met on our visit to Moscow and by their generally warm welcome to us. Is it perhaps not time for responsible American leadership to take a new look at the problems involved today in developing human resources? Furthermore, it seems imperative that the United States should devote a larger proportion of its energies and resources to the development of a new generation of Americans, who will have the skills and wisdom necessary for carrying out their responsibilities for leadership and cooperation in a new world of tomorrow.

EPILOGUE

We believe that the implications for Man, and his future, are obvious.

OBJECTIVE ELEVEN
(1964 to the present time)

To devise simple, practical, straightforward methods by which parents can actually promote both the growth of their children's brains and the increase of their children's intelligence.

Result

Such methods have been devised from 1964 to the present time. They have resulted in thousands of tiny children gaining markedly increased intelligence through early stimulation in learning to read, do mathematics, swim, play the violin, speak and read several languages, gain encyclopedic knowledge and a host of other things.

OBJECTIVE TWELVE
(1964 to the present time)

To teach parents of brain-injured children (these children had been diagnosed as mentally retarded or even as idiots) how to actually grow their children's brains.

Result

More than ten thousand families have been taught how to grow their hurt children's brains at The Institute for Physiological Excellence which is one of The Institutes for the Achievement of Human Potential. This Institute is directed by Mary Kett and is the senior Institute of The Institutes, having derived directly from The Rehabilitation Center at Philadelphia which was the original Institute. Roselise Wilkinson, M.D. is the Medical Director.

OBJECTIVE THIRTEEN
(1964 to the present time)

To determine whether parents could successfully take children with millions or billions of
dead brain cells and, by using the methods of
stimulating brain growth which we had taught
them, make such children function intellectually at an average, or even above average, level.

Result

*This has been accomplished by thousands of par-
ents of hurt children during the years 1964 to the
present time.*

OBJECTIVE FOURTEEN
(1964 to the present time)

To use the same knowledge and techniques which had been employed so successfully by parents in multiplying the intelligence of their brain-injured children, to multiply the intelligence of their own well infants and subsequently to measure the degree of success which would be achieved in tiny well children.

Result

Hundreds of parents of hurt children have applied the knowledge gained in growing the brains of their hurt children to their well infants and tiny children with equally fine results, thus making their well children even better in physical, intellectual, and social terms.

OBJECTIVE FIFTEEN
(1964 to the present time)

To compile all of the vast knowledge of brain growth and development in children which had been gathered over thousands of man-years of work on the part of the Staff and parents of The Institutes for the Achievement of Human Potential during the 40 years which elapsed between 1939 and 1979, and to organize the knowledge into an understandable program.

Result

This was accomplished and has resulted in the present day program which is known as "How To Multiply Your Baby's Intelligence".

OBJECTIVE SIXTEEN
(1964 to the present time)

To consider the knowledge gained thus far, i.e.——

1. The ability to take in raw data without effort is an *inverse* function of age.

2. It is *easier* to teach a one-year-old, one or many foreign languages than it is to teach anyone else, since all babies are linguistic geniuses.

3. It is *easier* to teach a one-year-old to read than it is to teach a seven-year-old.

4. It is *easier* to teach a one-year-old to do mathematics than it is to teach a seven-year-old.

5. It is *easier* to teach a one-year-old encyclopedic knowledge of birds, trees, flowers, reptiles, stones, fish, stars, minerals, history, presidents, kings, biblical characters, music, art, chemistry and a host of other subjects than it is to teach a seven-year-old.

6. It is *easier* to teach a one-year-old any set of facts than it is to teach a seven-year-old.

7. If you teach a tiny child the known facts on a subject he will intuit or discover the laws which govern them.

8. You can teach a child anything that you can present to him in an honest and factual way.

9. Learning is a survival skill.

10. Tiny children would rather learn than play with toys, play games or eat.

11. Mothers and fathers are the best teachers.

12. The brain literally grows by use.

13. Intense curiosity is a characteristic common to all geniuses.

14. Tiny children exceed geniuses in the intensity of their curiosity.

15. It is easy to make a child a genius *prior* to six years of age.

16. It is very difficult to make a person a genius *after* six years of age.

17. It is good, not bad, to be a genius.

18. Children who know the most and are the most effective are also the most delightful, charming, thoughtful and humane.

Result

This knowledge has been gathered, considered, evaluated, organized and used to improve the abilities of all children whose parents have requested such programs from The Institutes.

Various programs presently exist and are fully subscribed to by parents from many nations.

OBJECTIVE SEVENTEEN
(1964 to the present time)

To put the knowledge so far gained to more widespread use in improving the abilities and functions of tiny children from birth onward.

Result

Since 1964 the number of tiny children being made significantly more intelligent has increased in each successive year. This increase in growth had to be controlled by The Institutes due to The Institutes' lack of funds available for this purpose. The project has therefore had to be self-supporting in nature. This has made for growth which is slow but quite healthy with parents paying for services which they perceive quite correctly to be worth far more than the cost.

OBJECTIVE EIGHTEEN
(1969 to 1972)

To make more people aware that tiny children can be made superior by demonstrating that a significant number of profoundly brain-injured children could be made able to function normally. This was demonstrated by enabling paralyzed children to run, speechless children to talk, blind children to see and read and deaf children to hear, by the simple process of giving the child visual, auditory and tactile stimulation with increased frequency, intensity and duration in recognition of the orderly way in which the human brain grows. This in turn showed that *all* well children could obviously be made superior by doing the precise same things.

Result

In 1969 The Institutes agreed to permit a motion picture producer, John Goodell, to make a full length, technicolor, wide screen, 35 mm motion picture about the work of The Institutes. This film was completed by 1972 and won a nomination for the Academy Awards in 1974. The title of the film is Always A New Beginning.

THE SEVENTIES

OBJECTIVE NINETEEN
(1972 to 1973)

To organize completely the knowledge which had thus far been acquired as to how children take in information from birth to six years of age, how that information thus taken in results in immediate knowledge and how that brain stimulation actually results in brain growth and significantly higher intelligence.

To organize this knowledge into the most enjoyable and efficient methods possible in order to teach parents how to give their children vast knowledge of all subjects, resulting in brain stimulation, increased brain-growth and much increased intelligence.

Result

By 1972 it was abundantly clear to the Staff that it is possible to teach a tiny child absolutely anything which can be presented to the child in an honest and factual way. It was also abundantly clear that if you teach a one-year-old the facts *of a subject that he will discover or intuit the laws that govern that body of knowledge. Since this is the same method used by scientists to discover new laws it was clear that tiny children are themselves scientists in the truest sense.*

What was far less clear was precisely what are the actual facts of any given subject.

During 1972 and 1973 the Staff of The Institutes worked incessantly to determine the precise facts of a large number of subjects including mathematics, music, art, swimming, gymnastics, foreign languages and a host of others.

This study resulted in clear, straightforward methods and materials for teaching parents how to teach their babies and tiny children all of the above subjects and a host of others. Three vitally important books were written for parents to use as well as a great deal of teaching material to be used in teaching the children.

OBJECTIVE TWENTY
(1974 to 1975)

To demonstrate that it is both possible and easy to teach all tiny children to speak and read a foreign tongue by simply presenting the facts of the language, in the spoken and written form, to the child.

Result

During the years 1974 and 1975 five Staff members of The Institutes were dispatched to Tokyo to live in Japan and to teach tiny Japanese children, two to four years of age, how to understand, speak, and read English. This team, working with the Early Development Association of Japan, succeeded in teaching the Japanese children with the help of Japanese assistants. This team, under the leadership of Janet Doman and J. Michael Armentrout and later under the leadership of Douglas Doman (all of The Institutes' Staff) also gained invaluable experience in the teaching of well tiny children.

OBJECTIVE TWENTY-ONE
(1975 to 1976)

To create a new Institute of The Institutes for the Achievement of Human Potential. The new Institute to exist on the campus of The Institutes in Philadelphia. The purpose of the new Institute is to actually form a school for mothers and their newborn babies, the goal of which is to create tiny children who are intellectually, physically and socially splendid and who, as a result, function at levels two, three and more times higher than their chronological peers.

Result

In the Fall of 1975 a new Institute was formed under the direction of Janet Doman. This Institute is named "The Evan Thomas Institute" and teaches mothers how to teach their newborn babies how to speak, understand, read and write several languages including Japanese, Spanish, French, Portuguese, Hebrew and others.

The children of The Evan Thomas Institute, of whom there are approximately thirty and who range in age from newborn to four years of age, also read music, play the violin, do mathematics, swim, have encyclopedic knowledge on a host of subjects, write stories and

*poems, do Olympic routines and hold world champion-
ships in certain developmental functions such as creeping and brachiation.*

*These mothers and children attend The Evan
Thomas Institute several hours a week and carry on a
program at home. The program is carried out by the
parents under the direction of The Evan Thomas Institute.*

*The Evan Thomas Institute is visited by profes-
sional people and parents from every continent and the
tiny children have demonstrated their abilities to national network television audiences, at scientific seminars at NASA and to many distinguished visitors.*

*Most important of all, the children themselves are
not only intellectually, academically, physically and
socially far superior to their peers but are the most
charming, delightful, thoughtful and self-sufficient of
children.*

OBJECTIVE TWENTY-TWO
(1977)

To form a new Institute of The Institutes for the Achievement of Human Potential to exist on the campus in Philadelphia. The purpose of this Institute being to make the knowledge of how to multiply the intelligence of newborn babies and tiny children available to mothers in all nations who wish to know how to do so.

Result

The Better Baby Institute was formed in the summer of 1977 and is directed by Robert Derr. The Better Baby Institute performs its services to the children of the world in two ways:

1. *By the operation of* THE BETTER BABY PRESS *the purpose of which is to publish books and materials which instruct and aid parents in multiplying their babies' intelligence. These books and materials are made available at the lowest possible price so that they are within the reach of the largest possible number of parents, and in the largest number of languages.*

2. *To conduct lectures, seminars, and courses for parents on "How To Multiply Your Baby's Intelligence". These courses result in certi-*

fication as a Professional Mother or Father by The Temple Fay Institute of Academics which is an Institute of The Institutes for the Achievement of Human Potential directed by Neil Harvey, Ph.D.

OBJECTIVE TWENTY-THREE

(1977–1978)

To prepare an intensive course of seven days' duration to be taught to parents by the entire Staff of all of The Institutes for the Achievement of Human Potential. This course to make parents who attend capable of teaching their babies all of those things necessary to give their babies intellectual, physical and social superiority. The course to be presented as many times annually as demand on the part of parents dictates. The course to cover philosophical, historical and neurological background as well as the practical means of multiplying a child's intelligence including demonstrations by the children of The Evan Thomas Institute and instructions on how to prepare the necessary materials.

Result

The first course on "How To Multiply Your Baby's Intelligence" was presented to mothers and fathers from five nations in February of 1978 and since that time several hundred parents have received certification as Professional Mothers or Professional Fathers as a result of attending these courses. The parents who have attended these courses have each written a critique of the course. These critiques have been highly enthusiastic and glowing in nature. They abound with comments such as,

> *"The most important week of my life, not only as a parent but as a human being."*

> *"I've learned more about brain development in children than I learned in all of medical school."*

> *"This should be a required course for every black mother alive."*

> *"I realize now that I've been a 'closet mother'. This course has made me very proud to be a mother."*

The number of parent applications to attend the "How To Multiply Your Baby's Intelligence" Course grows larger monthly.

OBJECTIVE TWENTY-FOUR
(1979)

To create a properly licensed grade school to admit four-year-olds who have already been taught to read, write and speak at least two languages by their parents prior to admission. This school to act as a prototype for the schools of tomorrow.

This school to be an Institute of The Institutes for the Achievement of Human Potential, and be physically located on The Institutes' campus at Philadelphia.

Result

In January of 1979 The International School was created under the direction of Miki Nakayachi. The school is licensed by the Commonwealth of Pennsylvania for grades one through three. Additional grades will be added as they become necessary.

The curriculum of the school includes those subjects taught in the best grade schools in order that no holes should exist in the knowledge of the tiny children admitted. Those subjects normally covered in First Grade are covered along with much more advanced subjects during a three month period. This program permits nine additional months of highly advanced instruction in the First Grade.

Since all children admitted will already be highly competent readers prior to admission as well as being far advanced in a myriad of very sophisticated subjects and since the school will operate in trimesters there should be no difficulty in covering all subjects presently covered through High School as well as many subjects not covered in High School, prior to the Sixth Grade.

At the time of this writing (Fall of 1979) the school has been in operation for nine months. The students range in age from four to just six years of age.

The subjects already taught range from subjects normally taught in Third Grade to those normally taught in High School.

The students love the school and request constantly that the hours be increased.

(1979)

To prepare a plan by which a specific nation which wished to do so might raise significantly the intelligence of all of its citizens beginning immediately.

Result

In early 1979 the newly elected President of Venezuela, Presidente Luis Herrera Campins, took the far-sighted and entirely original action of appointing Luis Alberto Machado as the first Minister for the Development of Intelligence in history.

One of the Minister's early projects was to tour the world in order to see what, if anything, was being done to increase intelligence among the nations of the earth.

As part of that investigation, Minister Machado visited The Institutes in Philadelphia and intensive discussions were held during the week of May 7th, 1979, with the Minister, the Director and Staff of The Institutes, and Alberto Vollmer, the Vice President of The Vollmer Foundation.

Minister Machado requested that the Director of The Institutes prepare a detailed proposal by which The Institutes would contract with the Venezuelan government to raise significantly the intelligence of all Venezuelan children so that the Minister might then consider such a proposal.

After the departure of the Minister, the Director of The Institutes and The Institutes' Special Projects Team, drawing on The Institutes' vast accumulated knowledge of brain growth in children, completed this 99 page document by the 21st of May.

This document is known as The Venezuelan Plan *and a copy of this plan is available in the files of The Institutes.*

As a consequence of those discussions, the Minister and a group of Venezuelan professional people as well as two Directors of The Vollmer Foundation attended the seven day "How To Multiply Your Baby's Intelligence Course" presented by The Better Baby Institute on the Philadelphia campus of The Institutes for the Achievement of Human Potential from the 11th through the 16th of June, 1979.

At the conclusion of this course additional discussions were held between the Minister and his Aides, the Director and his Staff, and the Directors of The Vollmer Foundation. The Minister was presented with a copy of The Venezuelan Plan as were the Directors of The Vollmer Foundation.

At the present time (October 1979) the plan as well as other projects are under consideration by the Minister.

OBJECTIVE TWENTY-SIX
(The Present Time—October 1979)

To prepare a plan for the universal multiplication of intelligence, comprehensive enough to be used as the basis of a plan for:

1. A single family consisting of a mother, father, and child (population 3).

2. A small institute consisting of parents, children, and staff (population 100).

3. A very small community of people (population 200).

4. A small orphanage (population 500).

5. A small service club (population 1,000).

6. A village (population 5,000).

7. A geographical location (population 35,-000).

8. A small colony (population 50,000).

9. A trade union (population 1,400,000).

10. A state (population 4,000,000).

11. A small sized nation (population 9,000,-000).

12. A moderate sized nation (population 13,000,000).

13. A large nation (population 200,000,-000).

14. A large religion (population 700,000,-000).

15. A giant nation (population 800,000,-000).

The plan to provide for a significant increase in the intelligence of each child by an average of fifty percent over a period of three years for each newborn child resulting in vast savings in the cost of educating each child and the time required to do so.

Result

In June of 1979 Alberto Vollmer of The Vollmer Foundation called Glenn Doman, Director of The Institutes for the Achievement of Human Potential, and stated that The Vollmer Foundation was interested in the creation of a plan for the universal multiplication of intelligence and invited five Directors of The Institutes to Caracas for discussions and a series of lectures to various groups of leading Venezuelans including prominent people from government, industry, education, science, and business. Included was a lecture to twenty-eight Catholic Bishops.

This meeting took place in Caracas from July 8th to July 11th, 1979.

After intensive and mutually enthusiastic discussions between the Director of The Institutes and several Directors of The Vollmer Foundation including Gustavo Vollmer, the President, and Alberto Vollmer, the Vice President, the decision was made by The Vollmer Foundation to make a grant to The Institutes for the Achievement of Human Potential to support the cost of preparing such a plan.

The grant was in the sum of $31,600.00 and this plan is the result. The detailed plan follows.

Section III

The Present

the plan for

the universal multiplication
of intelligence

the plan for
the individual multiplication
of intelligence

Thousands of individual families have become aware that it is possible to multiply a baby's abilities in intellectual, artistic, physical and social terms and are determined to give their own children such opportunities immediately. Such families are quite unwilling to wait for group decisions to be made at organizational or governmental levels. These families come from every continent. They range from families of very limited income to wealthy families. They range from families with very limited educational backgrounds to families with most extensive educational backgrounds.

Such families have in common the fact that they are determined to give their own children the finest intellectual, artistic, physical and social opportunities and that they wish to do so immediately. This plan enables them to do so.

procedure for the individual multiplication of intelligence

This is the procedure to be followed by an individual family wishing to multiply the intellectual, physical and social abilities of its children.

1. The parents of a family gain knowledge, by whatever means, of the fact that it is possible to multiply the intellectual, physical and social abilities of its children who are six years of age and younger.

2. The parents determine whether they wish to do so.

3. The parents write to the Director of The Institutes for the Achievement of Human Potential stating that they wish to become Professional Parents and inquiring for information.

They write to:

> Glenn Doman
> Director
> The Institutes for the Achievement
> of Human Potential
> 8801 Stenton Avenue
> Philadelphia, Pa. 19118
> U.S.A.

In their letter of inquiry they request information as to how to become Professional Parents at:

a) *The Correspondence Level*
b) *The Attendance Level*
c) *The Residence Level*

The Director will then send them specific information about these three levels.

1. The Professional Mother (Father) Course at *The Correspondence Level:*

Parents enrolling in *The Correspondence Level* will be given options ranging from spending five minutes a day teaching their child to read to spending eight hours a day teaching their child (children) all skills. The costs will range from twenty dollars per year to one hundred dollars per year (1979). This level will result in a much more knowledgeable, intelligent and capable child, and for the parents a certificate of completion at *The Correspondence Level.*

2. The Professional Mother (Father) Course at *The Attendance Level:*

Parents enrolling in *The Attendance Level* will be given options ranging from spending one hour a day teaching their child everything to full-time teaching of their child (children). The total cost for this level is four hundred dollars (1979). This level will result in a very much more knowledgeable, intelligent and capable child, and for the parents a certificate of completion at *The Attendance Level.*

3. The Professional Mother (Father) Course at *The Residence Level:*

This course exists at two stages. Both stages require residency in or near the Philadelphia area.

a) Full time attendance at The Evan Thomas Institute on the campus of The Institutes for the Achievement of

Human Potential at Philadelphia, Pennsylvania, for the mother (father) and child. This course is for mothers and babies where the age of the baby ranges from birth to three years of age. The time involved with parent and child is all day, everyday. The time involved *at* The Evan Thomas Institute ranges from one hour per week for baby and parent to eight hours per week. The costs range from three hundred dollars per year to eight hundred dollars per year (1979). Parents who successfully complete *The Residence* Level at The Evan Thomas Institute will be qualified by certification as a Human Developmentalist at The Qualified Parent Level.

b) Full-time attendance at The International School for the child. This course also takes place on the campus of The Institutes and is restricted to children who have graduated from The Evan Thomas Institute at four to six years of age. This is a nine year program which contemplates a child bypassing High School altogether and entering College or University at 13 years of age having already covered all the subjects normally covered in High School plus others.

Upon receiving such inquiries from parents the Director of The Institutes will take the following steps:

1. He will respond to the parent inquiry by sending more detailed information to such parents as have inquired. This information will cover all three levels.

2. He will provide the parent with proper introductions to the appropriate Institutes' Director, depending upon which of the three courses of action the parents find to be of the greatest interest.

a) In the event that the parents express interest in *The Correspondence Level* he will provide introductions to the Director of The Better Baby Bookstore for materials to carry on the program without visiting Philadelphia as well as to the Director of The Institute for Intellectual Excellence who will be responsible to answer ongoing questions.

b) In the event that the parents express interest in *The Attendance Level* he will provide an introduction to the Director of The Better Baby Institute who will provide the parents with detailed information about the seven day "How To Multiply Your Baby's Intelligence" course which is conducted on the campus of The Institutes in Philadelphia, as well as information as to the next course in which a vacancy exists. (The waiting list varies from three to six months). During this course the parent will meet personally and receive instruction from the Directors of each of the nine Institutes, as well as the full faculty and Staff. Simultaneous translation is available for all courses in all major languages. The course materials such as books, are also available in most major languages.

c) In the event that the parents express interest in either of *The Residence Level* courses, the Director will provide introductions to both the Director of The Evan Thomas Institute and to the Director of The International School.

There is no charge for this correspondence, for materials supplied or for these introductions to facilitate further inquiry. The Institutes are a federally tax-exempt, non-profit organization and such information is a normal part of the services they perform for parents of all nations.

procedure for the universal multiplication of intelligence

This is the procedure to be followed by a group or nation wishing to multiply the intellectual, physical and social abilities of its people.

1. The governing body of a population of people gains knowledge, by whatever means, of the fact that it is possible to multiply the intellectual, physical and social abilities of its people.

2. Representatives of the governing body of the population request a meeting with the Director of The Institutes in order to:

a) Gain more knowledge as to how it is possible and why it is desirable to multiply the intellectual, physical and social abilities of its own population.

b) To explain to the Director how the interest in doing so came into being and why the governing body is interested in doing so.

3. If, at the conclusion of the opening conversations, the representatives of the governing body still wish to pursue the matter to the degree of gaining further knowledge and if the Director of The Institutes still wishes to pursue the matter to the degree of gaining further knowledge, the way is prepared for the next step.

4. The representatives of the governing body of the population return and report their preliminary findings to the governing body itself and determine whether the governing body wishes to take the next step in the procedure.

The Director of The Institutes simultaneously reports his preliminary findings to the Board of Directors of The Institutes for the Achievement of Human Potential to determine whether the Board of Directors wishes to take the next step in the procedure.

If either body determines that it does not wish to proceed further, the matter is closed.

If both bodies wish to proceed to the next step, the following acts are initiated——

5. The Director of The Institutes sets up a method by which a formal committee, established by the governing body of the particular population under discussion, can be fully informed as to how it is possible to multiply the intellectual, physical and social abilities of a population and why it is desirable to do so, along with the evidence of its long term results. Simultaneously the governing body sets up a high level committee of its own choosing with the ability, power and authority to take the next step. The Director of The Institutes establishes the charges The Institutes will make for the time, effort and knowledge which will be expended in supplying the information to the Blue Ribbon Committee of the governing group of the given population.

6. The agreed-upon orientation period will take place on the campus of The Institutes in

Philadelphia on the dates mutually suitable to the cooperating parties. The orientation meeting will require one seven day meeting followed by a three day discussion period. The entire program will therefore require ten consecutive days and nights of intensive study and discussion.

The seven days of orientation will consist of a totally planned and detailed presentation of philosophy, methodology, technology and demonstrations of how to multiply a tiny child's intellectual, physical and social abilities, including demonstrations by the children and mothers of The Evan Thomas Institute and The International School.

Following the seven day orientation and demonstration will be three days of detailed discussion of *The Universal Multiplication of Intelligence* Plan as described herein and how it would be specifically tailored to the precise population represented by the Blue Ribbon Committee.

These discussions will be between The Institutes' Selection Board and the Blue Ribbon Committee. The Institutes' Selection Board is composed of members of the Board of Directors and the Staff of The Institutes, and the Chairman of the Board of Directors of The Institutes.

7. The committee then returns to make its final report and recommendations to the governing body of the population under discussion and to seek its authority to make a binding agreement with The Institutes for the Achievement of Human Potential for the multiplication of the intellectual, physical and social abilities of its population within the broad terms of this Plan as it has been specifically tailored to meet the precise needs of that population.

8. The Selection Board of The Institutes and Staff makes its final report as recommendations to the Board of Directors and Staff of The Institutes for the Achievement of Human Potential and seeks its authority to make a binding agreement with the governing body to conduct a program which will multiply the intellectual, physical and social abilities of the population under discussion.

9. If both the governing body of the stated population and the Board of Directors and Staff of The Institutes for the Achievement of

Human Potential are in total agreement on *The Universal Multiplication of Intelligence* Plan as it applies to the population under discussion, the contract is signed and the program begins.

UMI method

To multiply the intellectual, physical and social quotient of each consecutively born child in a given population between birth and three years of age.

The program will require six consecutive years of time since it will deal directly with every baby born in that population during a three year period, and *for* a three year period. Thus if the program began with the first child born on the first day of 1980 and continued until the last child born on the last day of 1982 was three years old, the program would extend from January 1st, 1980 until December 31st, 1985.

This is to be accomplished when the governing body of a population of people has gained knowledge of the fact that this can be accomplished; that the consequences of doing so are entirely advantageous to the child, the family, the community, the nation and the world in humane, physical, economic, philosophical and all other terms; has actively sought and achieved the cooperation of The Institutes for the Achievement of Human Potential, Philadelphia, Pennsylvania, U.S.A., in doing so and has legally contracted with The Institutes to do so.

This program will begin by making all babies intellectually, physically and socially splendid over a three year period of time. It will do so by teaching the baby's parents precisely how to do so if, after knowing about it, they wish to do so.

THE FIRST YEAR
The First Day—January 1, 1980

1. At the onset of such a joint enterprise The Institutes will deliver to the governing body an initial program the purpose of which is to make the parents of that group aware that it is possible for parents to multiply the intelligence, the physical abilities and the social graces of their children and that the governing body of that population has elected to make the program available to all prospective parents within that population who wish to take advantage of that opportunity. This initial program

prepared and carried out by The Institutes will utilize television, radio, newspapers, magazines, mail, word of mouth, posters and all other means available to make known the fact that this opportunity is open to every member of that population. During this orientation period, the Director and other key Staff members will be available for interviews by the press, for feature articles in journals and magazines, for radio interviews and for dignified television talk programs, as well as supplying tapes and films of the children of The Evan Thomas Institute and The International School for use on public service television.

2. This orientation period will take six months starting on Day One of the first day of the six month program and continuing until the 182nd day (see SECTION III, The Present, "*UMI* Schedule"), and is known as the Initial Orientation Period.

All babies born during this same six month period would be eligible for the program as would all babies born during the second six month period of the first year. We will refer to these children as "Group One".

3. The parents who have found the information gained during the six month orientation period to be persuasive and who wish to give their child the opportunity to have multiplied intellectual, physical, and social abilities now indicate that they wish to do so by registering for the program itself. They do so by filling in a card available at all post offices and by mailing that card to the office designated by the governing body. Such parents will receive a prepared letter in response telling them precisely how and where they may now receive specific instructions as to how to multiply the abilities of their newborn baby.

The 183rd Day—June 30, 1980

4. At the beginning of the second six months of the first year, the Intensive Indoctrination Course at the Initial Parent Level will be given.

This Intensive Indoctrination Course is open to all women and men whose baby has been, or will be born during the year 1980. The program will be taught by the live Staff of The

Institutes to the live mothers and fathers if the population is small enough and geographical distances short enough so that the entire eligible population of mothers (and fathers where possible) can be gathered together, for a period of seven days, in a single place which offers the best possible auditorium facilities for intensive teaching purposes.

If the population is too large or the distances too great to make possible the gathering together of the entire population of parents for a period of seven days then television facilities of the highest order must be made available to the teaching faculty of The Institutes for a period of 48 hours and television broadcasts made available to all eligible parents. This program, whether live to a live audience or whether live to a television audience, will present the program listed in detail as follows:

Specific First Year Program

The Objectives of The Institutes—
Heredity and Environment

Babies: The Myth versus The Reality

Why You Should Teach Your Baby To Read

How To Teach Your Baby To Read

The Genesis of Genius—
How The Brain Grows

What Is Intelligence?
  a) Functional Intelligence
  b) Potential Intelligence

How You Create Intelligence

Bits of Intelligence

How To Teach Your Baby Bits of Intelligence

Mothers Are The Best Teachers—
It Is Good, Not Bad To Be Highly Capable

Teaching The Facts versus The Laws

Babies and Instant Math

How To Teach Your Baby Mathematics

The Spectrum of Neurological Organization

How To Make Your Child Physically Excellent

Demonstrations by the children and mothers of The Evan Thomas Institute and The International School.

a) This course will teach all mothers and fathers child development from birth until six years of age including slow development, average development, and superior development.

b) This course will teach the parents how to increase brain growth and function in intellectual, physical and social terms through stimulation.

c) This course will teach the parents the eighteen cardinal points of brain growth and development in babies.

d) This course will teach the parents that they *can* raise the intelligence of their children by showing the parents the film *Always A New Beginning.*

e) This course will teach the parents how to stimulate their own child's brain growth and to give their child, during his first year, encyclopedic knowledge on a host of subjects by supplying their child with thousands of individual facts known as "Bits of Intelligence" on a host of subjects including reading, mathematics, history, zoology, anatomy, music, biology, religion, astronomy and many others.

f) This course will demonstrate to the parents that all this can be achieved by presenting to

them the children of The Evan Thomas Institute speaking and reading several languages, playing the violin, demonstrating
their encyclopedic knowledge and ability to
solve problems, doing Olympic gymnastic
routines, swimming, etc.

g) This course will teach the parents specifically how to teach their baby to read prior
to twelve months of age.

5. Those parents who elect to actually carry
out the program with their child will be supplied with the following materials:

a) The book *How to Teach Your Baby to Read*
by Glenn Doman

b) The Glenn Doman *How to Teach Your
Baby to Read* Kit, Vol. I

c) Bits of Mathematical Intelligence (numbers One to Thirty-three)

d) Bits of Musical Intelligence (One to
Twenty)

e) Bits of Geographical Intelligence (One
to Twenty-five)

f) Bits of Geometric Intelligence (One to Twenty)

g) Bits of Zoological Intelligence (One to Twenty)

Special Note: These materials have a retail value of $50.00 (1979) and are included in the total charge to the governing body of the population. Since this charge, and those for the second and third years' material are already included in each year's costs, the governing body may choose to give these materials to the families without charge, or to recoup some or all of the cost of the entire program by charging the families for the materials used during the three-year program. The total retail value of the materials is approximately $600.00 (1979) for three years or twice the price of the total program.

6. The parents will receive additional Bits of Intelligence on varied subjects on the First of each month for the seventh, eighth, ninth, tenth, eleventh, and twelfth month. They will also receive additional instructions as to how to multiply their babies' social and physical abilities including crawling, creeping, and swimming.

The total value of the materials received during the first year will be approximately $200.00 (1979)

7. In order to insure that the program is being followed and as a healthy and desirable form of *quid pro quo* the participating parents will be required to fill out and return certain forms. These will report precise progress and which will provide an invaluable record available to both the governing body of the population and to The Institutes.

THE SECOND YEAR
The 366th Day—January 1st, 1981

8. At the beginning of the second year the same program will be carried out as has been outlined in points 1 to 7 for Group Two (those babies born between the beginning of the second year and the middle of the second year). Included in this program will be the pregnant mothers of babies who will be born between the middle of the second year and the end of the second year.

9. At the beginning of the second year the babies born in the first year of the program

(Group One) will range in age from newborns to one year of age. Thus the newest baby born will be beginning his first year of program. His mother will have been instructed six months earlier and will have received six monthly packages instructing her precisely how to proceed with him. A mother whose baby was six months of age when the first year of program began will now be one year old and will be clearly ahead of the average one year old in intellectual, physical, and social terms. How far ahead he is will be a product of the degree of time, love, skill and understanding of the program that his family has been able to bring to the child. The family will find itself a closer, more tight-knit and more loving group than ever before. The child's mother will have more material concerning what to do with him than she can possibly run out of during the next six months.

The 548th Day—June 30th, 1981

10. During the first week of this period two things will happen simultaneously:

a) The new second year group of new-borns' parents will receive their Intensive Indoctrination Course at the Initial Parent Level exactly as has been described in Step 4. This course will be followed with this second group of babies as described in steps 4 to 7 just as was the case with the first-year babies.

b) Group One babies will now range in age from six months to eighteen months. Their mothers will by this time be quite skilled in teaching their babies. They will therefore be ready for the second year Intensive Indoctrination Course at the Intermediate Parent Level.

11. The Intensive Indoctrination Course at the Intermediate Parent Level will be available only to those mothers who:

a) Are graduates of the Intensive Orientation Course at the Initial Parent Level, and————

b) Have successfully completed a minimum of six months of multiplying their baby's intellectual, physical and social growth.

12. The Intensive Indoctrination Course at the Intermediate Parent Level is also seven days long and will be taught by the faculty of The Institutes using the same means as were established initially to reach the parents.

Specific Second Year Program

Review of Human Development—
Birth to Six Years

How To Measure Your Baby's Intelligence—
The Institutes' Developmental Profile

How The Brain Grows (Intermediate Level)

How To Combine Bits of Intelligence

All Babies Are Linguistic Geniuses

How To Teach Your Baby A Second Foreign Language

How To Combine Bits of Mathematical Intelligence

How To Make Your Baby Physically Excellent

How To Teach Your Baby To Swim

Demonstrations by the children and mothers of the Evan Thomas Institute and The International School

a) This course will review child development from birth until six years of age and will add a course on fetal development from conception to birth.

b) This course will elaborate the developmental growth of brain and body taught a year earlier.

c) This course will teach the parents how to actually measure their own baby's progress on *The Institutes' Developmental Profile.*

d) This course will teach the parents an additional twenty-five cardinal points in brain growth and development of tiny children.

e) This course will teach the parents how to stimulate their child's brain growth even more than has already been done by elaborating the Bits of Intelligence which he has received and the number of subjects on which he is receiving encyclopedic knowledge.

f) This course will demonstrate to the parents what can be accomplished by parents working with their tiny children via additional demonstrations of The Evan Thomas Institute children, performing at even higher levels than those demonstrated a year earlier.

g) This course will teach the parents the fact that all babies are linguistic geniuses and will instruct them in how to begin to teach their babies at least one foreign language.

h) This course will elaborate the reading program of their children to include the reading of books in their own language and the reading of words in a foreign language.

i) This course will teach the parents how to begin teaching their children how to add, subtract, multiply, and divide based on the Bits of Mathematical Intelligence they have already received.

j) This course will teach the parents how to multiply their baby's physical growth by teaching running and brachiation.

13. Those mothers who have successfully carried out the program and have proven their eagerness to continue by having reported regularly on their child's progress will now be supplied with the following items either free or with a partial or total charge as has been decided by the governing body:

a) The Glenn Doman *How to Teach Your Baby to Read* Kit, Vol. II i)A book for assembly by the parent

    ii)The book *Goodbye Mommy* by Bruce King Doman

b) Bits of Foreign Language Intelligence (One to Twenty)

c) A foreign language tape

d) Bits of Mathematical Intelligence (Numbers 34 to 67)

e) Bits of Historical Intelligence (One to Twenty)

f) Bits of Chemical Intelligence (One to Twenty)

g) *The Path to Math* by Greta Erdtmann

These materials have a retail value of $50.00 (1979) and are included in the total charge to the governing body of the population.

14. The parents will now receive additional Bits of Intelligence on varied subjects on the first of every other month for the next year.

They will also receive sets of instructions on how to improve their baby's social and physical abilities including swimming.

The total value of these materials received during the second year will be approximately $200.00 (1979).

The 729th Day—December 31st, 1981

15. The first baby to begin the program is now two years old.

The last baby to begin the program as part of Group One is now one year old.

The 730th Day—January 1st, 1982

16. At the beginning of the third year the same program will be carried out as has been outlined in steps 1 through 7 for Group Three (those babies born between the beginning of the third year and the middle of the third year). Included in this program will be the pregnant

mothers of babies who will be born between the middle of the third year and the end of the third year.

17. At the beginning of the third year the babies born in the second year of the program (Group Two) will range in age from newborns to one year of age and thus will be beginning their second year of program. The same program will be carried out for them as has been outlined in points 8 through thirteen.

18. At the beginning of the third year the babies born in the first year of program (Group One) will range in age from two years to three years. These babies will be clearly superb in intellectual, physical, and social terms and their abilities will range from fifty percent higher than those of their peers (150 Intellectual Quotient, 150 Physical Quotient, 150 Social Quotient) to 300 percent higher than their peers (300 Intellectual Quotient, 300 Physical Quotient, 300 Social Quotient) depending on the tiny child's parents' ability to carry out the program. The child's family will be closer and more loving than has previously been the case and mutual respect between parents and child will be extremely high.

The 912th Day—June 30th, 1982

19. During the first week of this period three things will happen simultaneously:

a) The new third year group (Group Three) of newborn's parents will receive their Intensive Indoctrination Course at the Initial Parent Level exactly as has been described in Step 4. This course will be followed for the next year exactly as has been the case with Group One and Group Two.

b) Group Two will now range in age from six months to eighteen months of age. Their mothers will now be skilled in teaching their own tiny children and they will now begin their Intensive Indoctrination Course at the Intermediate Parent Level exactly as has been outlined in Steps 11 through 13.

c) Group One will now range in age from eighteen months to thirty months and their mothers will be highly efficient in teaching them in all areas of intellectual, physical, and social growth. They will now be ready for the third year Intensive Indoctrination Course at the Graduate Parent Level.

20. The Intensive Indoctrination Course at the Graduate Parent Level will be available only to those mothers who:

a) Are graduates of the Intensive Indoctrination Course at both the Initial and Intermediate Parent Levels, and——

b) Have successfully completed a minimum of eighteen months of multiplying their tiny child's intellectual, physical, and social growth, and——

c) Have demonstrated their degree of interest and enthusiasm by having reported progress to this point.

21. The Intensive Indoctrination Course at the Graduate Parent Level is also seven days long and will be taught by the Staff of The Institutes using the same methods as were established initially to reach the parents.

Specific Third Year Program

A Summary of Brain Growth and Human Development

How To Make Your Baby Physiologically Excellent

How To Give Your Baby Excellent Health Through Nutrition

Review of *The Institutes' Developmental Profile*— *The Profile* As A Diagnostic Tool

Programs of Intelligence

Programs of Mathematical Intelligence— Advanced Mathematics

How To Teach Your Baby A Second Foreign Language

How To Teach Your Baby To Write

How To Make Your Baby Physically Superior

How To Make Your Baby Socially Excellent

How To Teach Your Baby Music

Demonstrations by the children and mothers of The Evan Thomas Institute and The International School.

a) This course will complete the knowledge of brain growth and development from conception to six years of age and will expand the knowledge of nutrition in both a physical and intellectual sense stressing the best nutrition available in the particular geographical location of the population being dealt with.

b) This course will review how parents can measure their own baby's progress and degree of superiority on *The Institutes' Developmental Profile* and will also teach the parents to determine what areas need more and what areas need less attention.

c) This course will teach the parents the remaining 40 cardinal points in brain growth and development of tiny children.

d) This course will teach the parents all of the remaining knowledge necessary to stimulate their child's brain growth and to multiply the child's knowledge on a host of subjects and will also teach the parents how to teach their tiny children how to combine and permutate bodies of related facts in order to multiply almost infinitely the thousands of related facts they have already stored in their tiny child's brain.

e) The parents will be shown how their child's abilities have already been multiplied in intellectual quotient, physical quotient, and social quotient.

f) This course will demonstrate to the parents exactly what can be accomplished by parents working with their tiny children in The Evan Thomas Institute by final demonstrations on the part of the oldest children in The Evan Thomas Institute. The children demonstrating will be four years old.

g) The parents will be taught how to teach their own tiny children a foreign language.

h) The parents will be taught how to teach their own tiny children how to read all books in their own native language and complete books in at least one foreign language.

i) The parents will be taught how to teach their own tiny children how to do advanced mathematics.

j) The parents will be taught how to teach their own tiny children how to write in their own language and in at least one foreign language.

k) The parents will be taught how to teach their own tiny children Olympic gymnastic routines and how to accomplish physical superiority.

l) The parents will be taught how to teach their own tiny children social excellence within their own culture.

22. Those mothers who have successfully carried out the program will now receive the following materials:

a) *How to Multiply Your Baby's Intelligence* by Glenn Doman, Janet Doman, Susan Aisen, and the Staff of of The Evan Thomas Institute.

b) *Teach Your Baby Math* by Glenn Doman

c) Bits of Mathematical Intelligence (Numbers 68 to 100) plus mathematical formulas

d) *How to Make Your Baby Physically Superior* by Glenn Doman, Douglas Doman, Bruce Hagy, and the Staff of The Institute for Physical Excellence

e) *How to Teach Your Baby a Second Foreign Language* by Glenn Doman, Miki

Nakayachi, and the Staff of The International School

f) *How to Make Your Baby Physiologically Excellent* by Glenn Doman, Mary Kett, Roselise Wilkinson, Elaine Lee, and the Staff of The Institute for Physiological Excellence

g) *How to Make Your Baby Socially Excellent* by Glenn Doman, Gretchen Kerr, J. Michael Armentrout and the Staff of The Institutes

h) *How to Make Your Baby Musically Excellent* by Glenn Doman, Gail Engebretson, Miki Nakayachi, and the Staff of The Evan Thomas Institute

i) *How to Raise an Excellent Family* by Glenn Doman and Katie Doman

j) *How to Motivate Your Baby* by Glenn Doman, Gretchen Kerr, Janet Doman, Douglas Doman, Mary Kett and Roselise Wilkinson

k) *How to Give Your Baby Excellent Health Through Nutrition* by Roselise Wilkinson and Mary Kett

23. The parents will receive the above eleven books and booklets in the following way: six books at the time of the Intensive Indoctrination Course at the Graduate Parent Level and the remainder in the months that follow, not necessarily in the order listed.

The total value of these materials will exceed $200.00 (1979).

The 1,094th Day—December 31st, 1982

24. The first baby of Group One to begin the program is now three years old.

The last baby of Group One to begin the program is now two years old.

The 1,095th Day—January 1st, 1983

25. The first baby to begin the program is now just three years old and he graduates from the course. Depending upon how well, wisely and enthusiastically mother has carried out the program, he will range from a great deal better than he would have been if it had not been

done, through fifty percent above the average child if the program has been done poorly and inconsistently, to three hundred percent higher than the average child if the program has been done enthusiastically and consistently. This gives a range of Intellectual Quotient, Physical Quotient, and Social Quotient from 150 to 300, as defined elsewhere in this document. (See SECTION V, Explanatory Notes, "The Measurement of I.Q")

The three-year-old who graduates on this day now has a superb lead over the children who have not had the opportunities of the program plus a family who truly understands how to multiply intelligence and brain growth.

His family will be much closer, much more tightly knit, much more humane and much more loving. The entire family will be much better citizens of their population.

His parents now have the knowledge and ability to continue to multiply his abilities until he enters school able to read, able to write, able to do mathematics and with vast knowledge. He is now "school proof" to the degree that he will be neither a reading problem nor a learning problem. He has learned about how to learn.

At the very least he will have given his teacher additional free time to deal with the other less advanced children in his class who may have reading problems and learning problems while he continues to read and learn.

In the event that several children in his class have also had the same opportunity, his teacher will have even more time to deal with the children in the class who have had less opportunity.

In the event that all of the children in his class have had the same opportunity which he has had the entire class can simply move to subject matter several years ahead of the work that would normally be taught in the First Grade. The results of such a situation are discussed elsewhere in this book in SECTION IV, The Future, "The Results".

The 1,459th Day—December 31st, 1983

26. The last baby in Group One is three years old and graduates.

January 1st, 1984

27. The first baby in Group Two is three years old and graduates.

December 31st, 1984

28. The last baby in Group Two is three years old and graduates.

January 1st, 1985

29. The first baby in Group Three is three years old and graduates.

December 31st, 1985

30. The last baby in Group Three is three years old and graduates.

How to raise the intellectual, physical, and social abilities of babies is now in the folklore as well as the practices of the population under discussion.

The mothers who have already done this with their babies will have more babies and will without question give their new babies the same attention and opportunities as before using the same high quality materials still in their possession, and with vastly more experience than they had originally.

Raising superior children is now in the normal child-rearing procedure in that population.

The governing body of the population, state or nation will now have clearly brilliant and healthy children who will grow into superb adults.

Depending on the size of the population, its governing body will now be saving millions of dollars or even billions of dollars, which may now be devoted to solving other problems.

The cost of continuing to supply materials to future babies will now be reduced to an insignificant amount of money through negotiating with The Institutes for the rights to produce them within the community or to continue to purchase them through The Institutes at a small fraction of the retail price.

The untold wealth and answers to future problems which will be produced by a superb citizenry as succeeding ranks of children grow into adults is beyond knowing.

UMI schedule

YEAR ONE — GROUP ONE

January 1, 1980   — First baby in Group 1 is born

June 30, 1980   — First baby in Group 1 is six months old
— Last baby in Group 1 is minus six months old

December 31, 1980 — First baby in Group 1 is twelve months old
— Last baby in Group 1 is born

YEAR TWO — GROUP ONE

January 1, 1981   — First baby in Group 1 is twelve months old
— Last baby in Group 1 is one day old

June 30, 1981   — First baby in Group 1 is eighteen months old
— Last baby in Group 1 is six months old

December 31, 1981 — First baby in Group 1 is twenty-four months old
— Last baby in Group 1 is twelve months old

YEAR THREE — GROUP ONE

January 1, 1982 — First baby in Group 1 is twenty-four months old
— Last baby in Group 1 is twelve months old

June 30, 1982 — First baby in Group 1 is thirty months old
— Last baby in Group 1 is eighteen months old

December 31, 1982 — First baby in Group 1 is thirty-six months old
— Last baby in Group 1 is twenty-four months old

YEAR FOUR — GROUP ONE

January 1, 1983 — First baby in Group 1 graduates
— Last baby in Group 1 is twenty-four months old

June 30, 1983 — Last baby in Group 1 is thirty months old

December 31, 1983 — Last baby in Group 1 is thirty-six months old and graduates

YEAR ONE — GROUP TWO

January 1, 1981	— First baby in Group 2 is born
June 30, 1981	— First baby in Group 2 is six months old — Last baby in Group 2 is minus six months old
December 31, 1981	— First baby in Group 2 is twelve months old — Last baby in Group 2 is born

YEAR TWO — GROUP TWO

January 1, 1982	— First baby in Group 2 is twelve months old — Last baby in Group 2 is one day old
June 30, 1982	— First baby in Group 2 is eighteen months old — Last baby in Group 2 is six months old
December 31, 1982	— First baby in Group 2 is twenty-four months old — Last baby in Group 2 is twelve months old

YEAR THREE — GROUP TWO

January 1, 1983 — First baby in Group 2 is twenty-four months old
— Last baby in Group 2 is twelve months old

June 30, 1983 — First baby in Group 2 is thirty months old
— Last baby in Group 2 is eighteen months old

December 31, 1983 — First baby in Group 2 is thirty-six months old
— Last baby in Group 2 is twenty-four months old

YEAR FOUR — GROUP TWO

January 1, 1984 — First baby in Group 2 graduates
— Last baby in Group 2 is twenty-four months old

June 30, 1984 — Last baby in Group 2 is thirty months old

December 31, 1984 — Last baby in Group 2 is thirty-six months old and graduates

YEAR ONE — GROUP THREE

January 1, 1982	— First baby in Group 3 is born
June 30, 1982	— First baby in Group 3 is six months old — Last baby in Group 3 is minus six months old
December 31, 1982	— First baby in Group 3 is twelve months old — Last baby in Group 3 is born

YEAR TWO — GROUP THREE

January 1, 1983	— First baby in Group 3 is twelve months old — Last baby in Group 3 is one day old
June 30, 1983	— First baby in Group 3 is eighteen months old — Last baby in Group 3 is six months old
December 31, 1983	— First baby in Group 3 is twenty-four months old — Last baby in Group 3 is twelve months old

YEAR THREE — GROUP THREE

January 1, 1984   — First baby in Group 3 is twenty-four months old
— Last baby in Group 3 is twelve months old

June 30, 1984   — First baby in Group 3 is thirty months old
— Last baby in Group 3 is eighteen months old

December 31, 1984 — First baby in Group 3 is thirty-six months old
— Last baby in Group 3 is twenty-four months old

YEAR FOUR — GROUP THREE

January 1, 1985   — First baby in Group 3 graduates
— Last baby in Group 3 is twenty-four months old

June 30, 1985   — Last baby in Group 3 is thirty months old

December 31, 1985 — Last baby in Group 3 is thirty-six months old and graduates

UMI cost

1. Included in the cost, which is virtually all-embracing, are the following:—

   a) The total program.

   b) All instruction of the parents themselves.

   c) All instructions.

   d) All copyrighted and non-copyrighted materials necessary for the parents to use.

   e) The scientific knowledge upon which the program is based.

   f) The technical knowledge on which the technical aspects of the program is based.

g) The know-how on which the practical program is based.

h) The teaching knowledge of both parents and children upon which the methodology is based.

2. Factors not included in the cost:—

a) The means by which the parents are made aware that it is possible to multiply their own baby's intellectual, physical, and social abilities. (Posters, mail, radio, television, etc.) The software for such a program *is* included but the actual physical materials are not.

b) The governmental body of the population must supply the means by which The Institutes' team can reach all of the parents in the population who wish to multiply their baby's intellectual, physical, and social quotient. In groups of one thousand mothers or less this may mean the physical gathering of the mothers in a single suitable teaching area and in groups of more than one thousand this may mean through television, radio, newspapers, magazines or a combination of these.

c) Although The Institutes will supply all instructional material such as books, pamphlets, written instructions, teaching materials and other things that will be required by the parents for their children in the appropriate language and the cost of which is already included in the total costs, the governing body will be responsible for actually placing those materials in the hands of the parents themselves. In short, The Institutes will supply those materials into the hands of the governing body in the Capital city. It will be the responsibility of the governing body to distribute the materials by hand, through distribution centers, by mail or by other means to each individual family.

3. The cost of these services to a group, town, city, state, nation or other such population will be a hundred dollars (1979) per newborn child per year for each of three consecutive years; a total of six consecutive years will be

required to carry each child born in three consecutive years to the age of three.

Therefore, the total cost for each newborn child is $300 (1979) which is one hundred dollars per year per child.

As the number of newborn children a year in a given population increases, the cost per child per year will descend.

This table represents the total cost to a group or nation per child per year; per child for three years; and the total cost of the program:

UMI *Total Costs*

All costs which follow were computed as of the year 1979. Naturally it will be necessary to negotiate the costs individually at the time the contract is actually prepared.

Total Number of newborns per year	Cost per child per year	Total Cost per child over 3 years	Total Number of children	Total Charges for entire program
500	$100	$300	1,500	$450,000
625	$100	$300	1,875	$562,500
1,000	$100	$300	3,000	$900,000
5,000	$100	$300	15,000	$4,500,000
10,000	$90	$270	30,000	$8,100,000
20,000	$89	$267	60,000	$16,020,000
30,000	$88	$264	90,000	$23,760,000
40,000	$87	$261	120,000	$31,320,000
50,000	$85	$255	150,000	$38,250,000
60,000	$84	$252	180,000	$45,360,000
70,000	$83	$249	210,000	$52,290,000
80,000	$82	$246	240,000	$59,040,000
90,000	$81	$243	270,000	$65,610,000
100,000	$80	$240	300,000	$72,000,000
200,000	$79	$237	600,000	$142,200,000
300,000	$78	$234	900,000	$210,000,000
400,000	$77	$231	1,200,000	$277,200,000
500,000	$75	$225	1,500,000	$337,500,000
600,000	$74	$222	1,800,000	$399,600,000
700,000	$73	$219	2,100,000	$459,900,000
800,000	$72	$216	2,400,000	$518,400,000
900,000	$71	$213	2,700,000	$575,100,000
1,000,000	$70	$210	3,000,000	$630,000,000
2,000,000	$69	$207	6,000,000	$1,242,000,000
3,000,000	$68	$204	9,000,000	$1,836,000,000
4,000,000	$67	$201	12,000,000	$2,412,000,000
5,000,000	$65	$195	15,000,000	$2,925,000,000
6,000,000	$64	$192	18,000,000	$3,456,000,000
7,000,000	$63	$189	21,000,000	$3,969,000,000
8,000,000	$62	$186	24,000,000	$4,464,000,000
9,000,000	$61	$183	27,000,000	$4,941,000,000
10,000,000	$60	$180	30,000,000	$5,400,000,000

In the case of children whose parents are illiterate and who must therefore have help in teaching the baby, it will be necessary to negotiate each contract individually depending on number and percentage of parents who can not read, their location, accessibility and so on.

Section IV

The Future

the results

Most specifically the Plan will have its primary effect upon the following groups:

A. The Children
B. The Family
C. The Teacher
D. The School System
E. The Community
F. The Taxpayer
G. The Legislator
H. The Nation
I. The World

Upon all of these groups, the results will fall into two classes.

First: The accomplishment of excellence in the world's children; with all the rich rewards that excellence (and its offspring, creativity) in intellectual, physical and social terms have provided throughout history. Since time has begun art, science, medicine, business, commerce, in-

dustry, government and invention have flour-
ished, blossomed and borne great fruit from
the seeds that a handful of the great men and
women of the human race have produced. That
history of greatness has been marred by a series
of petty despots, criminals, tyrants and maniacs
who have succeeded in exploiting the fears, territorial instincts and predatorial behaviour still
written into a species so grand in potential as to
dare aspire to a sapience which is not yet totally
achieved. This has resulted in the creature
called Man, clever enough to kill hundreds of
millions of his own kind and yet not quite wise
enough to follow the teachings of love and
peace of the great teachers which Man himself
has produced.

In his brief history Man has produced a very
small number of truly great men, a large number of petty despots, criminally insane and
major despots and a vast number of basically
decent, reasonably intelligent human beings
capable of being led to great and good accomplishments but still vulnerable to being misled
into hatred and wholesale slaughter.

It is a great accolade that the example and the
teachings of the relatively small number of
great men and women have exerted sufficient

influence to permit us to survive our own ancient fears and instinctual behaviour.

It is an even greater virtue that the knowledge and wisdom we have gained has led us to the knowledge required to make ourselves truly sapient.

If, in the end, Man is to survive and to flourish in knowledge and wisdom, what is required is that all of humanity have the opportunity for knowledge, wisdom, and greatness so that we may produce a huge number of human beings who are wise, intelligent, loving and capable, not vulnerable to being misled by a smaller number of petty despots or tyrants.

This multiplication of intelligence can lead, not over centuries but over a small number of years, to a Golden Age of growth, prosperity and peace for mankind.

Such an opportunity now exists.

Second: The prevention of ignorance, illiteracy, learning problems and the reduction of the ravages of brain-injury leading to its ultimate elimination.

The savings in both human and economic terms are quite simply incalculable.

Here are the results for the family, group, village, city, state or nation which adopts the Plan:

A. THE CHILDREN

One-Year-Olds

As each set of parents learns how to give its newborn children the ultimate opportunity to develop in mobility, language and manual competence by giving these newborn children visual, auditory and tactile stimulation with increased frequency, intensity and duration, we will see one-year-olds who walk and run confidently, who swim, who read many words in several languages, who speak and understand phrases in several languages, who do simple mathematical problems quickly and accurately and who have many bits of intelligence on a number of subjects. They will also be more confident, more secure, more independent, more alert, more enthusiastic and more eager to learn than other one-year-olds. In short, these twelve-month-olds will have the capabilities of the most advanced 30-month-olds in the present society. Each child will have a functional I.Q. (see SECTION V, Explanatory Notes, "The Measurement of I.Q.") ranging from 125 to 250 depending on the degree of love, wisdom, and the frequency, intensity and duration with which the program has been presented to the child.

Two-Year-Olds

We will see two-year-olds who swim, run, climb, jump and perform physical feats far beyond their ages. These two-year-olds will speak in well-organized sentences in several languages and understand reasonably complex instructions and ideas in several languages. They will be capable of solving mathematical problems and simple equations very quickly and accurately. They will understand music, have perfect pitch and will have begun to play musical instruments. They will be capable of reading simple books in several languages with complete understanding and they will be capable of composing and writing legible letters in several languages. They will have encyclopedic knowledge on scores of subjects including history, art, music, science, geography, politics, botany, zoology, biology and anatomy. They will be capable of solving reasonably complex problems in semantics and logic. They will be charming, self-assured and independent and they will see adults as sources of information rather than as grown-ups to be bribed or blackmailed. Most important of all they will love to learn——in short, the two-year-olds will be as capable as the most advanced six-year-olds are presently. Each child will have a functional I.Q. (as defined within this book) ranging from 150 to 300 depending upon the degree of love, wisdom and the frequency, intensity and duration with which the program has been presented to the child.

Four-Year-Olds

We will see four-year-olds who swim, dive, do ballet, run three miles and who do Olympic routines with grace and skill. They will solve reasonably complex mathematical problems almost instantaneously and with complete accuracy. They will read virtually any book in their mother tongue with understanding and many books in foreign languages. They will read and write poetry and stories. They will read and write music and play at least one musical instrument well. Their understanding and use of spoken language will be virtually complete including an immense vocabulary. They will now have encyclopedic knowledge of hundreds of subjects and will be able to combine and permutate that knowledge to obtain new knowledge. They will have learned how to gain new knowledge by the independent use of reference material in libraries and elsewhere. They will have learned how to study a body of facts to determine the laws that govern that particular body of facts. They will be problem-solvers of the first water. They will understand the fundamental laws of science, physics, music, mathematics, physiology, chemistry, gravity, electricity and so on. They will be delightful and outgoing and will see themselves, not as helpless babies but as responsible members of a family with duties and responsibilities to the family and toward each member of it. They will have a keen sense of humor and enjoy jokes as well as humor which involves a play on words. They will be highly competent physically and capable of gymnastic feats beyond those of average adults and rivaling those of athletes. Most important of all, they will believe that learning is the most joyous and the most fascinating of all of life's games. In short, these four-year-olds will have the knowledge and abilities of present day twelve-year-olds and in many areas beyond.

Each child will have a functional I.Q. (as defined within this book) ranging from 150 to 350 depending on the degree of love, wisdom, and the frequency, intensity and duration with which the program has been presented to the child.

Six-Year-Olds

We will see six-year-olds who swim very well, who run six miles, who dive, dance and do ballet with great grace and skill. They will be clearly capable of competing for world championships in certain basic human developmental skills in which they have been given opportunity.

They will solve complex mathematical problems with a speed and accuracy which will leave adults bewildered.

They will read all books easily, skillfully and with pleasure. Their interpretations of books with multiple meanings such as Shakespeare, the Bible, the Koran, poetry etc. will be reasonable and perceptive and will be limited only by the number of experiences which it is possible to put into six joyous years.

They will write stories and poetry both skillfully and imaginatively.

They will deal skillfully and fluently in at least one foreign language including speaking, understanding, reading and writing.

They will have "broken the sound and sight barriers" and be comfortable in as many foreign languages as they have been exposed to, and in direct relationship to the frequency, intensity and duration with which they have been exposed.

They will read and compose music creatively, imaginatively and with some degree of skill. They will understand and appreciate music and they will possess perfect pitch. They will play at least one musical instrument skillfully and will be familiar with the characteristics and capabilities of all instruments in a full orchestra. They will understand the basic language of conducting orchestras.

Their understanding and use of spoken language will be extremely sophisticated and they will have extraordinary vocabularies often exceeding those of their parents. They will appreciate and enjoy language as a tool for pleasure, development and as a means of solving human problems.

They will be skilled at using reference material and at finding answers to questions. They will have acquired the knowledge, the skill and the ability to solve problems which they will apply skillfully to daily life and which will become an ingrained habit. This will result in an automatic problem-solving way of life.

They will have acquired an enormous and encyclopedic body of facts which will vastly increase their personal zest for life having, as they will, a much heightened awareness of, and understanding of, all which they see in the world around them.

They will have learned how to entirely conquer and assimilate a new subject by first breaking it down into bits of information (bits of intelligence); by next mastering those bits of intelligence; by next understanding the relationship between bits of intelligence; by next permutating the bits of intelligence; by next studying the facts (bits of intelligence) to determine the laws that govern that particular subject and finally to use the new knowledge so gained to achieve pleasure or treasure in whatever form, or both.

They will be charming, outgoing, humane, responsible and independent human beings and highly contributory citizens of the family and of the group.

They will be highly attuned to nature and to nature's creatures with humanity and respect for the dignity of each creature including that creature called Human.

They will be vastly enjoyable companions for adults and for each other with a keen awareness of others and a keen sense of humor far beyond their years.

They will be immensely alert.

In short, these six-year-olds will have the abilities and knowledge of present day fifteen-year-olds and in many areas beyond.

Each child will have a functional intelligence (as defined within this book) ranging from 150 to 400 depending on the degree of love, wisdom, frequency, intensity and duration with which the program has been presented to the child.

Nine to Twelve

We will see nine to twelve-year-olds who are physically, intellectually and socially superior to the degree of being unique in the world. They will be humane, dignified, sensitive, humorous first-rate human beings.

They will have all the knowledge, information, creativity and problem-solving ability of top flight high school graduates and most of them will have a great deal more.

They will be prepared to go directly to college or university and high school will be completely unnecessary for them.

They will be an important part of the world's answer instead of being a major part of the world's problem.

They will all be exceptionally high in an intellectual, physical and social sense.

They will range in I.Q. (as defined within this book) from 150 to 500 depending on the degree of love, wisdom, frequency, intensity and duration with which the program has been presented to the child.

The adults these highly advanced children will become will range in competence from the present-day highly selective classical description of genius which embraces not merely high scores on questionable intelligence tests but also as measured by lasting improvements in the world itself such as those left by Christ, Muhammad, Galileo, Leonardo DaVinci, Rembrandt, Shakespeare, Jefferson, Edison, Einstein and so on.

It would be unnatural not to ask, "And will there be no failures in this program?"

Of course there will be failures in the program but these failures will not be failures in the child. The failures which exist are clearly predictable and can, by their nature, be catalogued. Failures in degree will occur because of insufficient love of the child or of the objective to devote sufficient love, wisdom, frequency, intensity or duration to provide the necessary stimulation to the child. However, even these children will be a great deal better off than they would have been if the program had not been carried out at all. Their intelligence should, as a result, range from 110 to 150 (as defined within this book) rather than from 80 to 110 as would otherwise have been the case.

Total failure will occur when the child simply does not receive the program at all. This will be the case in the following circumstances:

1. Where the parents and child are totally isolated as is presently the case with many tribes in Brazil's Xingu territory.

2. Where the parents are, through no fault of their own, so totally ignorant as to have no knowledge worth passing on to a tiny child even when taught precisely how to do so.

3. Where the parents themselves are totally hostile and refuse to participate in the program for whatever reason.

4. Where the parents are simply emotionally or otherwise incapable of dealing with their own children in any way.

All of the situations listed will result in total failure in the program and all will exist to a greater or lesser degree in almost any society of large size which is likely to adopt this Plan. However, these people should represent a relatively small percentage of the population in any culture which is likely to wish to introduce this Plan in the near future (1980 to 1985).

The fact that a small proportion of a population will not be successful is neither a good nor a sufficient reason to withold its vast advantages from that much greater percentage of children who would benefit superbly from this program.

Indeed, the exact reverse is the case.

Since this program to multiply the intelligence of all children in a physical, intellectual and social sense is so vastly cheaper in economic, human and material terms than is the present incredibly expensive and virtually catastrophic failure, this will result in a huge amount of money, human and material resources being available from which large amounts may be concentrated on solving the problems of the small percentage of children whose parents are incapable of carrying out the program for whatever reasons. The Institutes are prepared with the knowledge and ability to solve these problems by special arrangements with the governing body in question.

The children who have been described might be described as Renaissance children who will grow into Renaissance men and women, thus initiating a new and Golden Age for the children of today and tomorrow.

B. THE FAMILY

The effect upon the family of having superb children will be in every way beneficial.

1. It is obvious that superiority eliminates the problems of inferiority such as the inability to read, learning problems and so on which are so expensive to a family in economic, human and social terms.

2. The pride which a family feels in having created superiority in its own children is the

strongest sort of pride which a family can give itself.

3. Not only is love between parents and children enhanced by the process of creating superior children but so is joy increased during the process. Perhaps most important of all is the fact that tremendous respect grows between parent and child as a product of the parent/child, teaching/learning process.

4. Family ties are greatly strengthened during the creation of superiority by the parent in the child. This process strongly favors the return to the family as the primary unit of society, a process which has been greatly weakened during the second half of the Twentieth Century.

5. Grandparents can be greatly strengthened in their relationship *with* the family and in their importance *to* the family by playing a direct role in the process of multiplying a tiny child's ability. The role of grandparents is often critical in multiplying a child's intellectual, physical and social abilities. This is especially true where it is absolutely unavoidable that the parents go out to work. Thus the grandparents who might otherwise feel unuseful and unwanted become of critical importance in teach-

ing the baby. Thus, also, does the family solve at once the problem of child and grandparent.

C. THE SCHOOL TEACHER

The primary problem which faces all school teachers is not the problem of the competent child, but is in fact the precise opposite. The teacher is daily obliged to spend a high percentage of her time, effort and energy on the incompetent child. A classroom without children who can't read, or can't do math, or can't learn must surely be the dream of every sane and competent teacher.

D. THE SCHOOL SYSTEM

For the precise same reason that the school teacher herself would be pleased by a classroom with all competent children (or even a higher number of competent children) so would the school system. In addition, the school system itself finds a disproportionate amount of its budget being spent on problem children (very often with little or no success to show for the large amount of money spent). Blessed indeed would be the school system which has neither special funds for problem children—nor any problem children.

E. THE COMMUNITY

For all of the reasons that the school teacher and the school system would welcome highly competent children rather than problem children, so would the community. Obviously children who have tremendous ability and are not only better children than children with problems but they also grow up to be better and more law-abiding citizens. Thus the community with brighter, more capable, more law-abiding citizens is also a community with more productive, more creative people who earn higher salaries, commit fewer crimes, require less police to protect other people from them, require less fire protection, pay higher taxes and are more responsible citizens.

F. THE TAXPAYER

Clearly the taxpayer is far better off with the creation of much more capable and knowledgeable children. The reduced costs of not having to pay huge taxes for school systems made uncommonly expensive by widespread reading problems, behaviour problems, discipline problems, learning problems and so on, is only the beginning of savings for the put-upon taxpayer. The elimination of high schools or even the reduction of the number of new high schools necessary to be built would, in and of itself, save the taxpayer many times the cost of *UMI*. The Plan could be paid for by the costs of the buildings alone. As every taxpayer knows, the cost of building a school is the least of the costs in running a school.

Nor would the vast savings in educational costs be the most important savings to the taxpayer. The savings in crime would be beyond calculating in economic terms as well as in human terms. Far less crime is committed by capable people than is committed by incompetent people who are made incompetent by school failures. While there are innumerable ways in which the taxpayers benefit from living in a population of more capable people, we will not list them but will add only the clear benefit to the taxpayer of being surrounded by highly competent people who will not need his help to support themselves and who will be more capable of helping to support others unfortunate enough to need help.

G. THE LEGISLATOR

A very proper complaint of the highly competent, conscientious and intelligent statesman at all levels of government, is that he or she is able to spend only a very small amount of time *acting* to improve the world because of the very large amount of time he or she must spend *reacting* to problems. It is obvious that children who are highly capable have fewer problems than children who are less capable. They thus present fewer problems that need to be solved by legislators at all levels. It is equally true that children who are truly highly capable grow into highly capable adults who do not look to government for the solution to their own problems but who are inclined instead to be both independent and self-sufficient. With a population consisting entirely, or almost entirely, of highly competent citizens the statesman could spend his time acting on opportunity rather than reacting to problems. So also could the president of a large corporation, or a large union, or any organization. An army of highly competent soldiers should certainly be the dream of every general. Just as an orchestra of highly competent musicians would be the dream of every superb conductor.

In fact, the wish to direct or to preside over a group of average or below average people could only be the wish of a fool, a weakling, a psychopath, or a dictator.

H. THE NATION

One becomes almost embarrassed to point out that a nation or group of highly capable people who had been highly capable in intellectual, physical and social terms since early childhood, would be a happier, healthier, wealthier, saner, safer, brighter, better, more humane nation than a nation composed of less capable people.

I. THE WORLD

The Institutes for the Achievement of Human Potential have been blessed, over their first quarter of a century of existence on the present campus in Philadelphia, with the privilege of having known many of the greatest human beings, thinkers, scientists, Nobel Prize winners, geniuses and workers of this century. To a man or woman, these truly superior human beings have been characterized by their humanity, warmth, humor, sanity, spirituality, decency, sense of fairness and love for other human beings.

Among the noble lessons the people who have been fortunate enough to be Staff members have learned over these long years, the following things stand out in glorious relief against a world not always sane, kind, gentle or wise:

The staggering potential which is inherent in every child born.

The true miracles which can be accomplished by parents with tiny children who they both love and respect.

That a world peopled by children, and subsequently by adults, who are truly intellectually, physically and socially excellent, will be a world free of war, insanity, dishonesty, hatred, violence, poverty and starvation which will have reached a place and an Age which is Golden indeed.

Section V

explanatory notes

random but vital considerations

In all of this Plan only one assumption need be made. This assumption is that knowledge leads to good and that ignorance leads to problems. If this is not true then all the assumptions of the modern world are untrue and the entire system is wrong not only in practice (which may well be true) but in philosophy as well. This Plan assumes that knowledge, intelligence, physical capability, social grace and humaneness are desirable and lead to good. All The Institutes' observations and results in ten thousand children confirm that conclusion.

There are no chauvinists at The Institutes either racist or nationalist, male or female. We love and respect all babies, boys and girls, mothers and fathers. To solve the maddening problem of referring to all human beings as "persons" or "tiny persons" we have decided in this Plan to refer to all parents as mothers and all little children as boys. It seems fair.

One problem that will arise among the uninitiated upon reading this volume will be the question as to whether creating a three-year-old of extraordinarily high abilities will necessarily result in a twelve-year-old or a thirty-year-old who is also superior. All of our results, all of the tests of which we are aware as well as all studies of genius of which we are aware, indicate that those who start ahead end up ahead. Indeed those who start ahead almost invariably widen the gap between themselves and others. Indeed at least one first-rate educator had the opinion that children who entered school already reading lost their advantage as time went by. Having conducted a longitudinal study, this scrupulous researcher reported fairly that those who started ahead stayed ahead. (See SECTION VI, Appendices, "Table of References")

Whenever there is a discussion of children performing functions far ahead of their chronological peers there is the suspicion that various forms of adult pressure, either overt or covert, are being applied to the child. There are two important facts to the contrary. The first is the experience of The Institutes and of others which is that it is not possible to pressure the tiny child's mind beyond that which brings it pleasure. Attempts on the part of adults to bring pressure on the immature brain simply cause it to tune out and turn the attention dial to another station. The second fact is that children who have the opportunity to learn would rather learn than eat or play, and all pressures are in the opposite direction with tiny children pressuring the adult with unlimited questions.

Finally, it is necessary to point out that this Plan is in no event a theoretical one. Every aspect has been designed, carried out and has produced positive results in thousands of children of dozens of nationalities, all major religions and all races.

to whom will the children be superior?

It is clear that it is neither desirable nor even possible to insist that parents give their babies or tiny children the opportunity to be intellectually superior.

This Plan proposes no such thing. Indeed, the Plan proposes that only parents who completely understand what is proposed and who enthusiastically enter into the proposal will succeed completely. Creating such understanding and enthusiasm is a vital part of the Plan itself.

It is a sad commentary that the world not only approves, but wildly endorses physical superiority and even physical conflict while being frightened by intellectual superiority and intellectual cooperation.

This worship of muscles and agility is abundantly clear in the worldwide love of football and other sports and reaches its epitome in the Olympics when hearts beat fast as three young people who have established themselves as the physical elite of the world stand on platforms of three heights while three national flags are raised, three national anthems are played and a gold, silver or bronze medal is hung about the necks of the three greatest athletes in the world in that particular physical activity and these three are proclaimed the three most elite in all the world.

This Plan is in no way an attack on physical prowess, sports or the Olympics. Quite the contrary—it incorporates physical superiority and teaches the children Olympic gymnastic routines.

These observations are merely to point out that while physical superiority and elitism are treasured, intellectual superiority and elitism are viewed with alarm by many.

A world which treasures muscle over brain has far to go.

This Plan proposes intellectual, physical, social and humane superiority but it does not propose an elite.

This Plan proposes intellectually, physically and socially superior children but it proposes about a billion of them. Since there are in the world about a billion children the question arises, "To whom will these children be intellectually, physically and socially superior?"

The Plan answers that question clearly. The children will be intellectually, physically and socially superior to themselves.

These one billion children will become, as the Plan progresses, four billion children who will grow into four billion adults or the entire population. It proposes things be, not as they are, but as they could be, should be and indeed must be if the world is to survive and improve. Man has changed the world around him to an incredible degree. The time has come and the knowledge presently exists for him to realize his most ancient dream which is to change himself for the better.

This Plan proposes precisely how to do that and outlines the result, not as a theory but as an existent fact. How fast it can occur will be a product of how quickly governing bodies can be found who are wise enough to understand that this can be done and courageous enough, or even self-serving enough, to take action on it and to reap the rewards for itself and their population.

Fortunately, few parents are among the people who are frightened by superiority. Indeed, parents have exactly the opposite fear. They are afraid that their children will be less than superior.

Still there are a small number of parents who are afraid of the thought of their children being intellectually superior. Not only is it true that this Plan will not be forced on them or their children, but it is impossible to do so, even if it were desirable.

The Institutes' Staff has had forty years' experience with ten thousand families and has gained much knowledge of reactions to proposals for creating superiority in children. It is true that these ten thousand families have been entirely self-selecting and highly motivated to improve their own children. It is also true that the vast majority of these children have been brain-injured and needed to be much improved intellectually, physically and socially if they were to function normally and to survive.

It is equally true that these families have come from more than thirty-five nations and every continent except Antarctica.

They have ranged from poor people to millionaires with the great majority being middle class in an economic sense.

They have ranged from people with no formal education to people with several doctorates.

It is also true that The Institutes have dealt with hundreds of families with well children who wished to make them better.

It is The Institutes' experience that when parents are made aware that programs exist to multiply the intellectual, physical and social abilities of their children, their reactions vary in the following ways:

1. The strongest and most favorable reactions come from families who range from low to upper income groups.

2. The weakest and least favorable reactions come from families of the very rich and the very poor although for very different reasons.

a) The majority of the very rich often feel that their children are already secure in intellectual, physical and social terms and feel the effort required is unnecessary and burdensome. They enjoy a false sense of security.

b) The majority of the very poor often feel suspicious and even that it is impossible to make their children superior. They suffer from a false sense of insecurity.

There are obviously exceptions to both a) and b). Some very rich families are among the most knowledgable and determined supporters of this Plan. Some very poor people are willing to make great sacrifices to give their children an opportunity for superiority.

3. Based upon its experiences and observations with children and families in a hundred and thirty-five nations The Institutes makes the following predictions:

That among the families of any given nation who are exposed to the Initial Orientation program——

a) Sixty percent of parents will enthusiastically support and joyfully enter into the proposed program.

b) Twenty-five percent of families will enter into the program with willingness but not enthusiasm and with some reservations.

c) Fifteen percent of families will not enter the program and their attitudes will range from skepticism to ridicule. Of these a small percent will be fearful or openly hostile.

4. After the first year on program—

a) Seventy percent of the parents will have become enthusiastic and will be successful.

b) Fifteen percent of the parents will remain willing and they will have been joined by ten percent of the parents who were initially skeptical but who saw the results being obtained in the children on the program, making ninety-five percent with results varying from good to excellent. This group will continue to improve in both enthusiasm and results.

c) This will leave a hard core remainder of five percent of children not on program for reasons of indifference, of antipathy, of psychosis, or of intractable stupidity on the part of their parents. These children will be forced to wait until the program is so engrained in the population that the system will itself contain the elements of the program.

the measurement of I.Q.

Precisely how I.Q. is determined and measured has been among the most carefully guarded secrets of all time. The psychologists and educators of the world have devised, utilized and hidden this secret from the parents of the world to whom it should be of the greatest concern. Parents have accepted this with relative calm both because they tend to accept the judgment of authorities and because the vast majority of parents have a fairly good idea of their own child's intelligence and abilities in any event.

Because this Plan deals with intelligence, because The Institutes have come over a period of forty years to the certain knowledge that the standard intelligence tests do not test intelligence, and because this Plan is written for the people of the world and not for psychologists and educators, this Plan proposes a simple and perfectly straightforward measurement of intelligence.

Since this Plan deals exclusively with children from birth to six, by which time (at six years) brain growth is essentially complete, it will utilize entirely the following measurement system:

The number 100 will represent average intelligence and ability in a child at any age in a modern culture whether European, American, Asian or African.

In most modern cultures a child is expected to take his first steps and to say his first words at about one year of age.

He is expected to be walking, understanding language and talking reasonably well by three years of age.

By about six years of age he is expected to walk, run and jump fairly well, to understand spoken language well and to speak it fairly fluently. He is also expected to begin to read and write his native tongue by six.

By twelve years of age he is expected to read and write his native tongue reasonably well, to have a fair grasp of mathematics and a number of other subjects and to have begun the study of a foreign language.

While all these abilities vary a bit from culture to culture they are all fairly well defined within a given culture by child rearing practices prior to six and by the school systems of a particular culture from six years of age until about eighteen years of age.

Physical abilities are also generally defined at various ages within a given culture.

This Plan will utilize 100 as a bare score for performance at a given age within a particular culture.

If a child is performing precisely with his chronological peers within his own culture he will be considered as having an intellectual, physical and social score of 100.

If a three-year-old is performing precisely like an eighteen-month-old in an intellectual, physical and social sense he will be considered to have an intelligence of 50.

If a three-year-old is performing precisely like a six-year-old in an intellectual, physical and social sense he will be considered to have an intellectual, physical and social intelligence of 200.

If a three-year-old is performing precisely like a three-year-old in physical terms, a four-and-a-half-year-old in social terms and a six-year-old in intellectual terms he will be considered to have a physical intelligence of 100, a social intelligence of 150 and an intellectual intelligence of 200.

And so on.

Section VI

appendices

biographies of the children

Frances Schutz

Frances began The Institute's program at two years of age in Switzerland. Her mother had attended the "How To Multiply Your Baby's Intelligence" Course and after receiving her certification decided to apply for entry into the program.

Frances is equally articulate in German and English. She also understands and speaks Italian, French and Japanese. Frances can read books in all five languages and usually insists on translating the language she is reading into one of her other languages as she goes along.

Recently, Frances has been entertaining her classmates and visitors to The Evan Thomas Institute with dramatic recitations from the works of William Shakespeare. Her "To Be or Not To Be" from *Hamlet* was vividly performed with feeling and clarity that astonished her audience.

Frances enjoys playing the violin and practicing the floor routines in gymnastics.

She paints and draws with precision and care. Recently she painted a scene of Mt. Fuji in Japan that demonstrated her patience and skill in this area.

Sean Katz

Sean began The Evan Thomas Institute's program at twenty-seven months, and has done well in every way. His achievements include being the youngest violin soloist chosen to play at the Suzuki National Convention held in Ithaca, New York, in 1978. Sean was four years old and played "Gavotte" by Bach, for an audience of over one thousand people.

In 1978 Sean was the youngest finisher in the Philadelphia mini-marathon, a four mile non-stop race for which he received a trophy. Although Sean finished well, his time would have been faster had he not slowed his pace and helped a less determined six-year-old to the finish line.

In May 1978, Sean won the World Championship, Tiny Kids Division, in Brachiation. He completed five consecutive trips, hand over hand on a ladder 18 feet in length and eight feet off the ground. His total distance was ninety feet non-stop.

Sean created his own gymnastic floor routine to Tschaikovsky's "Nutcracker Suite" when he was three years old.

In October of 1978, Sean and some of his classmates made their musical debut at the Academy of Music in Philadelphia. He was chosen to play with the touring Suzuki kids who are the best of over 6,000 violinists in Japan. The Suzuki students ranged from eight to fourteen years old, Sean was a scant five years old at that time.

Sean enjoys playing Bach, Schumann, Vivaldi, Beethoven, Mozart and Lully on his violin and recently said he would like to learn to conduct an orchestra as well.

Sean has performed on numerous occasions for The Institutes' distinguished guests. In May of 1977, he performed at the joint meeting of NASA Scientists and The Institutes' Human

Developmentalists, where he shared the po-
dium with Nobel Prize winner Linus Pauling.
Sean read a book, conversed in Japanese,
demonstrated some gymnastic skills and played
his violin for America's leading scientists.

In the summer months, Sean enjoys camping
and hiking in addition to his other activities. At
the end of last summer he was filmed diving
into a full size swimming pool, fully clothed,
and backstroking the full length of the pool. He
is working towards his Junior Lifesaving Certificate. Sean enjoys reading and has read as many
as 100 books in a week.

Marc-Mihai Dimancescu

Marc-Mihai began The Evan Thomas Institute's program at the age of three. Within
months, Marc-Mihai was reading in both English and French, and now enjoys a book
equally well in either language. Also at three
years of age, Marc-Mihai introduced his classmates (two and three-year-olds) to neuro-
anatomy and neurophysiology, by giving a brief
talk on the subject. He illustrated his points

with diagrams of the human brain, locating parts and their functions to his youthful audience.

Marc-Mihai performed with his classmates on the stage of the Academy of Music in October of 1978. He performed three selections on the violin with total aplomb and remarked afterward that it was almost as exciting as sleeping in a bunk-bed.

In the spring of 1977, Marc-Mihai performed before the country's top scientists at NASA along with nine other Evan Thomas Institute students. He read in three languages (English, French, and Japanese), played his violin, and identified several modern space vehicles by name, using scientific terminology which delighted the audience.

Marc-Mihai spent the summer of 1978 touring France with his family and wrote a journal of his adventures in the cities and countryside. Highlights of the journal were comments on his favorite works of art and national landmarks.

Brandi Katz

Brandi began as an Evan Thomas Institute student at nine months of age. With her older brother, Sean, at her mother's side as a model and teacher, Brandi has excelled in every way.

She was three years old when she performed at NASA's Ames Research Center, Moffett Field, California. Brandi spoke in Japanese, played her violin, read in English and performed an intricate balance beam routine that demonstrated her agility and spatial awareness.

As a tiny little girl, Brandi's fondest wish was to have her own library card. Ridiculously enough, one must be able to sign one's name in a small space at the bottom of the library card. Brandi's signature was clear but large so initially she was denied a card. She overcame her disappointment and practiced diligently to be able to sign her name in the tiny space. When she arrived at the library and announced she could now apply for her card and had brought her own pen to sign, the librarian insisted she use the library's pen. Brandi was not used to this pen so she took it home and went back to practicing. A week later she marched in and signed her card, much to the shock of the librarian. She was two years old at at the time.

From three years of age on, she has written a diary of her daily adventures which is rich in detail of her very full life. Brandi writes in both English and Japanese.

She was the youngest student of The Evan Thomas Institute to appear at The Academy of Music in 1978. It was no surprise she had achieved this so early as she began to play the violin at thirteen months.

Brandi can be seen daily at the Y.M.C.A. near her home where she jogs two and a half miles non-stop.

Brandi celebrated her fourth birthday in March of 1979. Three days prior to her birthday, an article about her many achievements was published nationwide. The article was carried by *Ripley's Believe It Or Not.*

Micah Sherman

Micah began The Evan Thomas Institute's program at three years of age.

Today, Micah understands and reads fluently in both English and Spanish, and easily translates one language into the other for listeners. In addition, Micah understands, reads and speaks Japanese, Italian, and French.

He enjoys music very much and began composing his own works before his fourth birthday. He has put several of his favorite poems to music and is compiling quite a collection of his own music.

Micah performed with his classmates on the stage of the Academy of Music in October, 1978, to a crowd of over one thousand Philadelphia music lovers and was received with much delight and applause for his three violin selections.

At three years of age, Micah was also performing complicated gymnastic floor and balance beam routines which were modeled after the Olympic routines. His enjoyment, skill and grace were much admired by all.

Micah is equally at home in either Philadelphia, Pennsylvania, or Barcelona, Spain, where he spends his summers. He makes the transition between the two cultures without difficulty and always contributes in some way in either environment. Micah enjoyed touring the great cathedrals, museums and historic landmarks in Barcelona and wrote to his classmates of the fine art, music and history he was enjoying.

Recently Micah was asked what privilege in school he would like to achieve and his response was to be able to teach the younger children.

Harry McKinney

Harry McKinney began The Evan Thomas Institute's program with his mother at the age of two and a half years. Although a native Philadelphian, Harry quickly began to learn to read and understand Japanese and today can read several elementary level Japanese books, as well as identify hundreds of the ancient Kanji characters. Harry very much enjoys reading English as well and has been reading the newspaper and reporting to his classmates on current events since he was four years old. He plays the violin, the xylophone and the piano and enjoys improving his skills on all three instruments.

Harry also enjoys mathematics very much and plays games with his mother with both square roots and fractions in an algebraic way. Harry likes his mother to produce a solution for which he readily supplies the problem.

Socially, Harry has always demonstrated a maturity beyond his years. Because of this he is presently one of the senior students in his class.

Donna Pallas

Donna began The Evan Thomas Institute's program at the age of three and a half years. Today, at the ripe old age of five years, she is quite accomplished at many skills. Donna reads in both English and Japanese. She is an expert in ornithology and enjoys nothing better than reading a new book on this subject. Donna can play both the violin and the piano. Her other musical interests include musical composition and singing harmony. She enjoys writing and drawing, in fact she completed her first oil painting at the age of four. Donna is also an accomplished young gymnast. She has excelled on the balance beam and is equally at home doing floor routines. She has also learned modern, folk and tap dancing and has just begun learning formal ballroom dancing.

She can be as tough on the track as she is graceful on the dance floor when she leads her teammates in two-mile runs through Philadelphia's Fairmount Park.

In addition to her busy schedule, Donna has large responsibilities as the eldest of four girls in her family. Since all the Pallas girls are studemts in The Evan Thomas Institute, Donna is a vital part of the teaching environment at home. She actively teaches her three younger sisters, helps care for them and independently handles many household jobs so that her mother can teach her little sisters.

the mothers of the evan thomas institute

Each mother is carefully chosen from the many who apply. This Institute is designed to teach Professional Mothers. Professional Mothers are defined as those mothers who have as their top priority the expansion and development of their children's abilities.

Each mother is chosen for her enthusiasm and energy as a Professional Mother. The vast majority of the programs taught to the children are subjects that are not familiar to the mothers. The Evan Thomas Institute mothers learn Japanese, violin, Olympic gymnastics and a host of scholarly subjects not included in any average education.

These mothers are having a second and far more comprehensive education than the first time around.

table of references

This Table of References is provided for those readers who wish to have additional information on the subject of multiplying the intelligence of children. The books and articles referred to here may be ordered from:

THE BETTER BABY PRESS
8801 Stenton Avenue
Philadelphia, Pa. 19118

Individual Staff members of The Institutes are also referred to for those readers who wish to ask specific questions about some area of The Institutes' work.

OBJECTIVE ONE

Chapter Two, *What to Do About Your Brain-Injured Child,* Glenn Doman; Doubleday & Co. (1974)

Also published by Jonathan Cape, London (British Empire) and available in the following foreign language editions:

Germany —Hyperion Verlag, Freiburg
Hebrew —Bezalel Tcherikover, Tel Aviv
Italian —Armando Armando, Rome
Japanese —Simul Press, Tokyo
Portuguese —Grafica Auriverde, Ltda., Rio de Janeiro

Temple Fay, M.D., James M. Wolfe, Ed.D.; Charles C. Thomas Co. (1968)

OBJECTIVE TWO

Chapters Four and Five, *What to Do About Your Brain-Injured Child,* Ibid

OBJECTIVE THREE

Chapter Eight, *What to Do About Your Brain-Injured Child,* Ibid

The Institutes' Developmental Profile, Glenn Doman and the Staff of The Institutes; THE BETTER BABY PRESS (1962)

OBJECTIVE FOUR
Chapter Thirteen, *What to Do About Your Brain-Injured Child,* Ibid

OBJECTIVE FIVE
"Decade of Discovery", *What to Do About Your Brain-Injured Child,* Ibid

Human Neurological Organization, Edward B. LeWinn, M.D.; Charles C. Thomas Co. (1969)

Brain Injured Children, Evan Thomas, M.D.; Charles C. Thomas Co. (1969)

OBJECTIVE SIX
Chapter Thirteen, *What to Do About Your Brain-Injured Child,* Ibid

OBJECTIVE SEVEN
"Introduction" by Raymundo Veras, M.D.; *What to Do About Your Brain-Injured Child,* Ibid

Adventures with the Missing Link, Raymond A. Dart, M.D.; Institutes Press (1959)

Children of Hope, Children of Dreams, Raymundo Veras, M.D.; Henry Regnery Co. (1975)

African Genesis, Robert Ardrey; Atheneum (1969)

OBJECTIVE EIGHT

Introduction, *How to Teach Your Baby to Read,* Glenn Doman; Random House (1964)

Also published by Jonathan Cape, London (British Empire) and Pan Books, Ltd., in Australia and New Zealand, and available in the following foreign language editions:

Afrikaans	—Stimulus, Johannesburg
Dutch	—De Beziga Bij, Amsterdam
French	—Editions Retz/C.E.P.L., Paris
German	—Hyperion Verlag, Freiburg
Greek	—Elefterios A. Daskalakis, Athens
Hebrew	—Bezalel Tcherikover, Tel Aviv
Italian	—Armando Armando, Rome
Japanese	—Kodansha, Tokyo
Portuguese	—Jose Olympio Editora, Rio de Janeiro
Spanish	—Aguilar, S.A., Madrid
Swedish	—Evangeliska Fosterlands, Stockholm

Arabic and Icelandic editions in preparation.

OBJECTIVE NINE

How to Teach Your Baby to Read, Ibid

OBJECTIVE TEN

The work of David Krech, Boris Klosovskii, and a host of other neurophysiologists in stimulating the brains of laboratory animals is available at all large libraries.

Autoradiographic Examination of the Effects of Enriched Environment on the Rate of Glial Multiplication of the Adult Rat Brain, Joseph Altman and G.D. Das; *Nature* 204:1161–1163, (1964)

Moscow in May, 1963: An Interchange of Soviet and American Ideas Concerning Education, Programmed Learning and the Human Mind, Oliver J. Caldwell and Loren R. Graham; U.S. Department of Health, Education and Welfare, Office of Education. (1964), Supt. of Documents Catalogue No. 5.214:14106

Information per se, Paul S. Henshaw; *Nature,* 199:1050–1052, (1963)

The Development of the Brain and Its Disturbance by Harmful Factors, B.N. Klosovskii; Pergamon Press, Oxford, (1963)

Environmental Impoverishments, Social Isolation and Changes in Brain Chemistry and Anatomy, David Krech, Mark R. Rosenzweig, and Edward L. Bennett; *Physiology and Behavior,* 1:99–104, (1966)

How to Teach Your Baby to Read, Ibid

Teach Your Baby Math, Glenn Doman; Jonathan Cape, London (1979)
Simon & Schuster, U.S.A. (1980)

This book will also be available in the following foreign language editions:
Afrikaans —Stimulus, Johannesburg
Hebrew —Bazalel Tcherikover, Tel Aviv
Italian —Armando Armando, Rome
Japanese —Simul Press, Tokyo
Spanish, Portugese, French, and other languages to follow.

What to Do About Your Brain-Injured Child, Ibid

The Institutes' Philosophy, Glenn Doman and the Staff of The Institutes; THE BETTER BABY PRESS (1965)

OBJECTIVE ELEVEN
The Institutes Report, Editor—Pearl LeWinn; Published bimonthly by THE BETTER BABY PRESS

The New Parentage, Editor—Lee Pattinson; Published bimonthly by THE BETTER BABY PRESS

The "How To Multiply Your Baby's Intelligence" Course; Presented periodically by The Better Baby Institute

OBJECTIVE TWELVE

The ten thousand records of the children who have been programmed by The Institute for Physiological Excellence contain literally billions of carefully measured data concerning neurological, physical and intellectual growth of brain-injured children.

Results are published bimonthly in the "Victories" section of *The Institutes Report.*

OBJECTIVE THIRTEEN

The "Victories" section, *The Institutes Report,* Ibid

OBJECTIVE FOURTEEN

The reference for this Objective is the families of The Institutes.

OBJECTIVE FIFTEEN
How to Multiply Your Baby's Intelligence (Brochure); THE BETTER BABY PRESS

OBJECTIVE SIXTEEN
Janet Doman, Associate Director
The Institutes for the Achievement of
Human Potential
8801 Stenton Avenue, Philadelphia, Pa.
19118

OBJECTIVE SEVENTEEN
Robert Derr, Director
The Better Baby Institute
8801 Stenton Avenue, Philadelphia, Pa.
19118

OBJECTIVE EIGHTEEN
The film *Always a New Beginning*
Robert T. Stevens, President
Noramcom, Inc.
1421 Broadview Drive, Glendale, Calif.
91208

OBJECTIVE NINETEEN
Teach Your Baby Math, Ibid

How to Multiply Your Baby's Intelligence, Glenn Doman, Janet Doman and Susan Aisen; In press (1980)

How to Raise an Excellent Family, Glenn Doman and Katie Doman; In manuscript

OBJECTIVE TWENTY
Janet Doman, Associate Director
The Institutes for the Achievement of Human Potential
8801 Stenton Avenue, Philadelphia, Pa. 19118

OBJECTIVE TWENTY-ONE
Susan Aisen, Director
The Evan Thomas Institute
8801 Stenton Avenue, Philadelphia, Pa. 19118

OBJECTIVE TWENTY-TWO
The Better Baby Bookstore
8801 Stenton Avenue, Philadelphia, Pa. 19118

OBJECTIVE TWENTY-THREE
The Registrar
The Better Baby Institute
8801 Stenton Avenue, Philadelphia, Pa.
19118

OBJECTIVE TWENTY-FOUR
Miki Nakayachi, Director
The International School
8801 Stenton Avenue, Philadelphia, Pa.
19118

OBJECTIVE TWENTY-FIVE
J. Michael Armentrout
Director for Special Projects
The Institutes for the Achievement of
Human Potential
8801 Stenton Avenue, Philadelphia, Pa.
19118

OBJECTIVE TWENTY-SIX
The Director
The Institutes for the Achievement of
Human Potential
8801 Stenton Avenue, Philadelphia, Pa.
19118

PROCEDURE FOR THE UNIVERSAL MULTIPLICATION
OF INTELLIGENCE, *UMI* MATERIALS:

First Year——

1. The book *How to Teach Your Baby to Read* by Glenn Doman

2. The Glenn Doman *How to Teach Your Baby to Read* Kit, Vol. I

3. Bits of Mathematical Intelligence (numbers One to Thirty-three)

4. Bits of Musical Intelligence (One to Twenty)

5. Bits of Geographic Intelligence (One to Twenty)

6. Bits of Geometric Intelligence (One to Twenty)

7. Bits of Zoological Intelligence (One to Twenty)

Second Year——

1. The Glenn Doman *How to Teach Your Baby to Read* Kit, Vol. II, including:

   a) A book for assembly by the parent

   b) The book *Goodbye Mommy* by Bruce King Doman

2. Bits of Foreign Language Intelligence (One to Twenty)

3. A foreign language tape

4. Bits of Mathematical Intelligence (numbers Thirty-four to Sixty-seven)

5. Bits of Chemical Intelligence (One to Twenty)

6. The book *The Path to Math* by Greta Erdtmann

Third Year——

1. *How to Multiply Your Baby's Intelligence* by Glenn Doman, Janet Doman, Susan Aisen and the Staff of The Evan Thomas Institute

2. *Teach Your Baby Math* by Glenn Doman

3. Bits of Mathematical Intelligence (numbers 68 to 100) plus mathematical formulas

4. *How to Make Your Baby Physically Superior* by Glenn Doman, Douglas Doman, Bruce Hagy and the Staff of The Institute for Physical Excellence

5. *How to Teach Your Baby a Second Foreign Language* by Glenn Doman, Miki Nakayachi and the Staff of The International School

6. *How to Make Your Baby Physiologically Excellent* by Glenn Doman, Mary Kett, Roselise Wilkinson, Elaine Lee and the Staff of The Institute for Physiological Excellence

7. *How to Make Your Baby Socially Excellent* by Glenn Doman, Gretchen Kerr, J. Michael Armentrout and the Staff of The Institutes

8. *How to Make Your Baby Musically Excellent* by Glenn Doman, Gail Engebretson, Miki Nakayachi and the Staff of The Evan Thomas Institute

9. *How to Raise an Excellent Family* by Glenn Doman and Katie Doman

10. *How to Motivate Your Baby* by Glenn Doman, Gretchen Kerr, Janet Doman, Douglas Doman, Mary Kett and Roselise Wilkinson

11. *How to Give Your Baby Excellent Health Through Nutrition* by Roselise Wilkinson and Mary Kett

RANDOM BUT VITAL CONSIDERATIONS
Children Who Read Early, Dolores Durkin; Teacher's College Press, New York (1966)

RECOMMENDED READING

Books——

How to Teach Your Baby to Read, Glenn Doman; THE BETTER BABY PRESS

What to Do About Your Brain-Injured Child, Glenn Doman; Doubleday

Teach Your Baby Math, Glenn Doman; Simon and Schuster

Adventures with the Missing Link, Raymond Dart, M.D.; Institutes Press

African Genesis, Robert Ardrey; Dell

Brain-Injured Children, Evan Thomas, M.D.; Charles C. Thomas

Brain Child, Peggy Napear; Harper & Row

Children of Dreams, Children of Hope, Raymundo Veras, M.D.; with David Melton; Henry Regnery Co.

How to Teach Your Baby to Swim, Claire Timmermans; Stein and Day

Human Neurological Organization, Edward B. LeWinn, M.D.; Charles C. Thomas

I Think I Can, William Bresky; Doubleday

Kindergarten Is Too Late!, Masaru Ibuka; Simon and Schuster

King Solomon's Ring, Konrad Lorenz; New American Library

Let's Cook It Right, Adelle Davis; New American Library

Let's Get Well, Adelle Davis; New American Library

Let's Eat Right to Keep Fit, Adelle Davis; New American Library

Let's Have Healthy Children, Adelle Davis; New American Library

Nurtured by Love, Shinichi Suzuki; Exposition Press

On Aggression, Konrad Lorenz; Bantam

Suzuki Changed My Life, Masaaki Honda, M.D.; Summy-Birchard Company

Todd, David Melton; Dell-Laurel Edition

The Human Zoo, Desmond Morris; Dell

The Naked Ape, Desmond Morris; Dell

The Territorial Imperative, Robert Ardrey; Dell

Vitamin C and the Common Cold, Linus Pauling; W.H. Freeman and Co.

When Children Need Help, David Melton; Independence Press

Articles——

A Bill of Particulars on Seizures and on Discontinuing Anti-Convulsant Drugs, Edward B. LeWinn, M.D., F.A.C.P.; THE BETTER BABY PRESS

The Institutes Report, Editor—Pearl LeWinn; published bimonthly by THE BETTER BABY PRESS

The Institutes' Philosophy, Glenn Doman and the Staff of The Institutes; THE BETTER BABY PRESS